RUTH BADER GINSBURG

RUTH BADER GINSBURG
THE LAST INTERVIEW
and OTHER CONVERSATIONS

 MELVILLE HOUSE
BROOKLYN • LONDON

CONTENTS

INTRODUCTION

Perhaps the reason Ruth Bader Ginsburg flourished in the face of adversity was the circumstances into which she was born, on the Ides of March in 1933—the child of an immigrant in the middle of the Great Depression. Raised in the Flatbush section of Brooklyn, her Russian-born father was a furrier at a time when people stopped buying furs, and her mother, the child of Polish immigrants, worked in a garment factory. When young Joan Ruth Bader—she would become Ruth in grade school due to a preponderance of Joans—was only fourteen months old, her six-year-old sister Marilyn died of meningitis. Her mother died the day before Ruth graduated from her public high school.

Seeking to fulfill her mother's wish that she become a teacher, Ginsburg went on to Cornell University. "No one ever expected me to go to law school," she later explained to *The New York Times* in one of her first public interviews, contained herein. "I was supposed to be a high school teacher, or how else could I earn a living?" While at Cornell, she would study with Vladimir Nabokov, who, she would tell Bill Moyers in another of this book's interviews—the last interview of her life, in fact—would have a profound influence on the writing style that would later draw acclaim in her court decisions.

Ginsburg graduated the highest-ranking woman in her class, and soon after married her classmate Martin Ginsburg, who had graduated a year earlier and gone on to law school. After giving birth to her daughter Jane—Ginsburg's pregnancy had led to her demotion in a job she'd taken with the Social Security Administration—she enrolled at Harvard Law School, one of only nine women in a class of over five hundred men. When Martin got a job at a law firm in New York, she transferred to Columbia Law School, where she would graduate tied for first in her class.

Her brilliant performance in school didn't help her get a job very quickly, however. No law firm would hire her, and when she sought a clerkship with Supreme Court Justice Felix Frankfurter, he turned her down because she was a woman. Eventually, she got a teaching position at Rutgers Law School, but she had to accept a lower salary than the male professors.

In 1972, Ginsburg moved on to teach at Columbia Law School, where she became the first woman to achieve tenure, and she also founded the Women's Rights Project at the American Civil Liberties Union. As director, she argued six

landmark gender discrimination cases before the Supreme
Court, winning five—effectively eradicating gender discrimination from most areas of American law. Her reputation quickly soared and in 1980 President Jimmy Carter
appointed her to the U.S. Court of Appeals for the District
of Columbia—a "precedent-setting move," as she observed in
a conversation with high school students contained herein,
"that became a pattern," whereby subsequent presidents began more regularly appointing women to the bench.

By the time of her elevation to the Supreme Court in
1993, Ginsburg had become known not only for her legal bril-
liance, but also for her ability to build consensus with more
conservative judges, such as her Appeals Court colleague Antonin Scalia (who by that time had also been appointed to
the Supreme Court). Appointed by President Bill Clinton,
she was only the second woman ever to serve, and the first
Jewish woman.

She would go on to write many of the court's more historic
decisions, such as that of *United States v. Virginia*, which struck
down the male-only admission policy of the Virginia Military
Institute. She would also become known for some withering
dissents, such as in *Shelby County v. Holder*, which—as she details herein in an interview with journalist Jane Eisner—"cut
the heart out of the Voting Rights Act of 1965."

In her later years, especially as the Court became more
conservative and she was, for several years, its only woman,
Ginsburg's fame took on a new level in popular culture.
In 2013 a law student's Tumblr account about her dubbed
her "The Notorious R.B.G.," after fellow Brooklynite, rap-
per The Notorious B.I.G. The name stuck, and books and

documentaries about her appeared more and more regularly. People delighted in stories about how she chose which white lace jabot to wear over her judicial robes (it depended on whether she was issuing a dissent or a majority opinion); about her workout regime; about her close friendship with her polar opposite on the Court, Antonin Scalia; and her passion for opera. There was even an opera written about her friendship with Scalia. (Scalia himself comments on their friendship herein, saying about her "What's not to like? Except her views on the law.")

Opera, in fact, was the career she would have chosen if she could do it all over again, she told her friend, National Public Radio legal reporter Nina Totenberg. "In my dreams, a recurring dream is I'm onstage at the Metropolitan Opera, and I'm about to sing *Tosca*, and then I remember that I am a monotone!"

The outpouring of grief upon her death from pancreatic cancer in September 2020 bespoke a nation filled with a deep gratitude that she was a monotone, and even in death she broke one final glass ceiling: Ruth Bader Ginsburg was the first woman to lie in state in the Capitol of the United States.

RUTH BADER GINSBURG

COLUMBIA LAW SNARES A PRIZE IN THE QUEST FOR WOMEN PROFESSORS

INTERVIEW BY LESLEY OELSNER
THE NEW YORK TIMES
JANUARY 26, 1972

In a new accelerating competition among the nation's law schools, Columbia University has just scored a major coup: its law school, to its undisguised glee, has just bid for and won a woman for the job of full professor—the first in its 114-year history.

The glee comes in part because the woman, Ruth Bader Ginsburg, is what the school's dean, Michael Sovern, calls "so distinguished a scholar" that her credentials and honors would stand out in any catalogue of professors.

It comes too, as University of Michigan Law School dean Theodore St. Antoine says, at a time when many of the country's best law schools have been "scrambling" for women, often for the same ones. Most have no women at any rung of the professorial ladder, and, according to other sources, the woman Columbia got was among those being scrambled for.

And the glee is likely to spread far beyond the Columbia law faculty and into the law schools, where women students have long sensed an anti-female bias.

The appointment of Mrs. Ginsburg does not add to the handful of women now working as full professors of law, for she has been a full professor at Rutgers, the State University of New Jersey, since 1969. It does, however, mark the first time that Columbia Law has chosen a woman for a full-time post higher than lecturer, or part-time post higher than adjunct professor.

SEVERAL WOMEN CHOSEN

Beyond that, it coincides with the selection this winter of women by a few equally well-regarded schools, including Stanford, the University of California at Los Angeles, and Yale, as assistant or associate professors. All the appointments are, as in Mrs. Ginsburg's case, subject to approval by the governing boards of the respective universities and effective next fall.

The deans say that the search for women, begun a couple of years ago but intensified considerably since then, is now underway from Harvard to Indiana University to Stanford. A major reason for this new effort, the deans said in interviews, is the increased number of women now coming out of law school, now about 10 percent of the graduates and growing. The lack of available women in the past, they said, was the reason for the present paucity of female faculty members.

But there were other reasons offered for the present effort too, ranging from the demand by the increasing number of female law students for female professors to an appreciation of the benefits of a diversified faculty, to the "realization," in Mr. St. Antoine's words, that "law is a profession that a woman can handle as well as a man"—or, as Murray Schwartz of UCLA put it, to the fact that "whatever bias or prejudice or whatever you'd call it by the male faculty against hiring women" has disappeared.

PHILOSOPHICAL ATTITUDES

Professor Ginsburg, for her part, takes a philosophical stance—pleased with some of the progress to date and delighted to be going to Columbia, but anything but Pollyannaish as to prospects for future change.

In an interview she recalled that when she graduated from Columbia Law she was tied for first place in her class.

But she could not get a job with a law firm, she said. At first, when the rejection notices started coming in, she thought something might be wrong with her, but then, she said, "when I got so many rejections, I thought it couldn't be they had no use for me—it had to be something else."

So she got, upon graduation, a job clerking for a Federal district judge—whereas, as anyone familiar with the subject knows, and as she refrained from pointing out, a man with those grades from that school could have gotten a clerkship in a Federal appeals court, if not the United States Supreme Court.

Later she went to Rutgers, where, for her first few years, she feels, there was some discrimination. That stopped after a while, she said, but last fall, as a visiting professor at Harvard Law, giving a course involving women's rights, she noticed a little of the same male wariness there too.

"The law teachers are like that mostly," she said, feeling that the women's movement "threatens a way of life they find very comfortable."

What does she expect, and how will she act, she was asked, when she goes to Columbia this fall to teach procedure, conflicts, and a special course, in conjunction with the American Civil Liberties Union, on sex discrimination?

Said Professor Ginsburg, the 38-year-old wife of a successful tax lawyer and mother of a girl, 16, and a boy, 6: "The only confining thing for me is time. I'm not going to curtail my activities in any way to please them."

"I don't think I'll have any problem," she added a moment later. "People will be pleasant on the outside. Some of them may have reservations about what I'm doing, but I don't think they'll be expressed."

At any rate, her new role is far from what was expected of her in her girlhood, when, she recalled: "No one ever expected me to go to law school. I was supposed to be a high school teacher, or how else could I earn a living?"

INTERVIEW WITH U.S. COURT OF APPEALS FOR THE DISTRICT OF COLUMBIA CIRCUIT JUDGE RUTH BADER GINSBURG

INTERVIEW BY CONNIE DOEBELE
C-SPAN JUDICIAL AFFAIRS
MARCH 28, 1986

CONNIE DOEBELE: Judge Ginsburg, how did you come to be a judge on the US Court of Appeals?

JUSTICE RUTH BADER GINSBURG: I was nominated by President Carter and confirmed by the Senate. I was, for many years before my appointment, a law teacher, first at Rutgers Law School, part of the State University of New Jersey, [and then] from 1972 to 1980 at Columbia Law School. I was also an active litigator for what I call equal rights for men and women.

DOEBELE: Why was it important for you to become a judge, or did you always want to be a judge?

GINSBURG: I wanted to be active in the law. The law is a consuming love for me, and I've enjoyed everything that I've done in it—lawyering, teaching, and now judging. I didn't think specifically about becoming a judge, because frankly, I didn't think it was possible.

DOEBELE: Why?

GINSBURG: At the time I started to teach, you could count on one hand the number of women holding jobs at the professorial level in law schools. There were then no women at the Court of Appeals level, no women at all. Then Shirley Hufstedler was appointed in the sixties, and she remained [the only] one, until President Carter. So it seemed to me an area in which women were not yet wanted.

DOEBELE: What do you think changed in our society or in the judiciary to make it possible for a woman to become a judge in the US Court of Appeals?

GINSBURG: It wasn't just our society. It was something that started to happen in the sixties all over the world, some places faster than others. It was the notion that women should become fully participating members in society, full citizens. And at the same time men should become more involved with their families and that it would be healthier for people if children had two parents, not just one, and that we would take best advantage of all of our talent if we included women among our doctors, lawyers, even Indian chiefs.

DOEBELE: Were you surprised when you were appointed?

GINSBURG: I don't think it's fair to say that I was surprised. I was elated that the Carter Administration made a concerted effort to appoint women to the judiciary. He had made several appointments in 1979, so by that time the situation that existed throughout the sixties and most of the seventies had been radically altered. There were women on the bench. Carter was appointing them in numbers, so then at that point, I could aspire.

DOEBELE: You talked a little bit about the precedent, and President Carter's nomination of you. Is it important, to a judge, as to who nominates them, and whether that president is a Democrat or Republican, liberal or conservative, are they branded as that kind of judge?

GINSBURG: It should make no difference at all to a judge's performance, and perhaps the public has a misunderstanding about that. Federal judges are appointed for life, or as the Constitution says, "during good behavior." A federal judge has an obligation to do justice fairly and equally to all parties who come before the court, and never to allow a thought about what pleases the home crowd to influence that judge's decision. So it should make no difference whether a judge is appointed by President Reagan, or was appointed by President Carter, to the quality of the decisions that that judge is making on the court.

DOEBELE: You say it shouldn't. But does it?

GINSBURG: Very rarely. I think that most people—in the federal courts at least—when they put on the robe, know that they have the security, that they are in office for life and that if they vote as the law and justice demand, they won't be voted out of their position for doing that. So I think most judges do recognize the tradition, the importance of the job they're doing, and for them to do that job with total impartiality.

DOEBELE: You talked about your love for the law. What kind of personal satisfaction do you get from being a judge?

GINSBURG: The law is something that I think I deal with well. I don't have the kind of talent that could make one, say, a great opera singer—that's a wonderful natural gift. But there's something about working with the law, to help make society more rational, to help perhaps make people's lives a little better, it is something—the law is a stabilizing influence in society. It says these are the rules of the game, this is how we operate, we settle our disputes amicably, not through the use of violence.

DOEBELE: When a case comes to you, what's the general process that you personally go through to decide on it?

GINSBURG: I study cases very hard before the day in court. I read the decision in the trial court if it came to us from a court or, the decisions from the agency, if it came from an agency. My law clerks help me research all the decisions that bear on this one, and then I get together a set of questions to ask counsel on all points in the case that are unclear to me, and I ask those when the case is argued before the panel of the judges.

DOEBELE: How important is the prior briefings, the prior work that a lawyer does, versus that lawyer's performance verbally to you, the day it comes before you?

GINSBURG: The written work is what endures. The oral argument is fleeting. We have fifteen, twenty, tops thirty minutes a side for oral argument. I regard oral argument as a very important kind of "hold the line" operation. Oral argument is more important for retaining a victory than for obtaining one. I can put it this way: I have seen some cases that started out as winners on the basis of the written work turn out to be losers after oral argument, but I have seen only two cases where something that the judges viewed as an unsatisfactory, a losing case turning into a winner, only twice in five and a half years.

DOEBELE: And is that the oratory of the lawyer that comes through?

GINSBURG: It's—no, it has nothing to do with the lawyer's style. It has to do with the clarification that comes out in response to the judge's question, something that we didn't understand accurately about the case.

DOEBELE: Judge Ginsburg, is it difficult for you to put your personal attitudes aside when you go to rule on a case?

GINSBURG: No, and if I thought my personal attitudes affected how I would judge a case, I wouldn't sit on that case.

DOEBELE: You have that option not to?

GINSBURG: I think you have the obligation not to. If you come to a case with a predisposition, that you feel you cannot judge it impartially, you should not sit on the case.

DOEBELE: Are there any issues that, although you may not have personal strong feelings about [them], you say, "Gee, I wish I never have to work on this issue again, I'm so tired of it."

GINSBURG: I can't say that I feel that way about any issue that comes before our court. I think we have what I describe as a fast-moving feast. We have such a diversity of issues, cases from the agencies, from the trial court . . . even the agencies [are] different in their subject matter, so one day we may be hearing from the Nuclear Regulatory Commission, and the next day from the National Labor Relations Board, and the next day from the Environmental Protection Agency, and the next day from the Food and Drug Administration. The business is so varied, that I don't tire of having the same diet, not at all.

DOEBELE: What kind of personal pressures do you come under for being a judge on this level?

GINSBURG: It's a job that requires a lot of work to be done in a satisfactory way, so that you don't have much time for outside activities. People are sensitive when they talk to you because the conversation may turn to an issue that's in a case that has come before us. So, lawyers are very careful, and we have to be careful too at cocktail parties not to say anything that will indicate something about a case that is pending before the court.

DOEBELE: Is it difficult to have close friends in those cases?

GINSBURG: No. I think I can distinguish my personal friendship with a lawyer from anything that lawyer may be presenting in court. Lawyers and judges in this country are friends; they do talk to each other, they're the members of the same bar associations. That's quite different from the way it is, say, in Europe, where there is a line between judging and lawyering. You decide when you graduate from law school whether you want to be a judge or whether you want to be a lawyer. And you pursue a judicial career or a lawyering career. Judges and lawyers do not mix in bar associations, say, in France or in Sweden. But in this country judges have always been chosen from the practicing bar, so there's an understanding and a rapport in the way we select judges and the way judges deal with and relate to lawyers.

DOEBELE: You talked about not much time for much else, and you do have a family.

GINSBURG: Yes. I have a husband and two children.

DOEBELE: Is it tough to make time for them?

GINSBURG: They don't require time right now because my daughter is thirty and my son is twenty. I hope very soon that I will be able to make time for a grandchild that's on the way.

DOEBELE: So, one of the things that's been discussed has been your workload. One of the issues that is before the Supreme Court and different issues before the court is the possibility of a new level of federal court to take off some of the load. What is your opinion on that?

GINSBURG: I think we don't need a new level of court. We have three levels and that's quite enough. What we do need is the removal of some cases. We have too many cases. Too much is coming before the court and I think that throwing more judges at the problem is simply not the answer. The federal courts should be kept close to their current size. It's dangerous to go beyond the size we are now. This court has twelve judges authorized. The collegial relationship diminishes if we get beyond that size. We become a different kind of an institution. There are cases that don't have to come to this court—that don't have to come before judges at all. In my view, Congress should concentrate on taking out of the system cases that do not require, or disputes that do not need to be handled, as federal cases.

DOEBELE: Can you give me an example.

GINSBURG: Well there is one special court that I would support, and that is a special court to hear tax appeals. We now have one circuit, the federal circuit, that gets all appeals in patent cases. Expertise is important and valuable in that area. I think the same can be said for tax cases. Then the federal courts do a whole business in what's called diversity of citizenship cases. Cases come to us simply because the parties are from different states. An ordinary automobile accident that has nothing to do with federal law can come to this court, or come to our district court first and then to us on appeal if one party is from Maryland and the other party is from the District of Columbia. That is not a rational way to allocate business between local and federal courts. If you took away that diversity business—diversity of jurisdiction business— from the federal courts that would reduce our case load some

15 to 20 percent. And that's the direction in which I think Congress should go, and not to enlarge the federal judiciary.

DOEBELE: Let's talk specifically about this level of the judiciary. Why is the US Court of Appeals so important?

GINSBURG: It's important in the sense that most cases that come here and are decided here stay decided as we have decided them. That is, very few of our cases are accepted by the Supreme Court for review—our review of the decisions of agencies or of trial courts. Our review is not a matter of discretion. Parties who lose the agency before the district court are entitled to come here as a matter of right. But you don't get to the Supreme Court as a matter of right. So most parties don't bother even to appeal our decisions, and the few that do try to get to the Supreme Court overwhelmingly fail. So, we are the final instance in close to 99 percent of the cases we decide.

DOEBELE: Have you ever had one of your cases overturned?

GINSBURG: Oh yes, yes.

DOEBELE: How does it feel?

GINSBURG: The cases that get overturned are controversial cases. There's no personal insult or embarrassment if, say, the Supreme Court overturns one of our decisions with a 5–4 vote. That vote itself shows that the case was close and controversial. In many areas the law is not clear and certain. And there are ambiguities. You exercise your best judgement to attempt to fathom, say, what Congress meant when it wrote a statute that's very hard to understand. So, every judge in the system tries to do his or her best job. I certainly hope that district judges that we reverse or the agency decision makers that we reverse don't take a reversal on a personal level. These are very hard questions.

DOEBELE: Would you ever pick up the phone and say to a judge on a different or on a lower level, "Gee, I'm sorry I had to overturn that but I really felt this way"?

GINSBURG: No, we never discuss that.

DOEBELE: Is that a matter of ethics or you just don't do it?

GINSBURG: I wouldn't describe it as a matter of ethics but I think more as a tradition. We've said what we think about the judgement that we're reviewing in our opinion, and we don't pat the decision makers on the back if we think they've done a fine job either. Whatever our judgement is it's just there to be read.

DOEBELE: Some say that this is the second most important court—this circuit is the second most important court next to the Supreme Court. Do you agree?

GINSBURG: I think that the courts on our level—the federal courts of appeals—are all important. This one gets more government business, or perhaps people think of it that way.

Others get more commercial business. It is a very important court. All the federal courts of appeals are important.

DOEBELE: You always sat on a three-judge panel?

GINSBURG: Yes.

DOEBELE: Is that easier or harder than sitting alone or sitting with nine justices?

GINSBURG: It's more challenging.

DOEBELE: Why?

GINSBURG: Because you can never do anything alone, you must always carry at least one other mind to decide a case. If you can't persuade at least one of your colleagues, then you end up being a dissenter. So there is a psychological aspect to this job as well as a legal aspect, that is, you must not only be satisfied yourself that you have determined the law correctly but you must be in a position to persuade your colleagues that that decision is right. The one-judge court—the district judge—has a hard job and the rulings must be made on the spot at a trial. And the judge in the middle of a trial has no opportunity to rush up to the library, to check a book before he or she makes a ruling. But in our court, we listen to arguments, we don't issue our decisions immediately—there is time to think and research the issue. To that extent, the job in a court of appeals is easier because you don't have to make instant, immediate decisions. On the other hand, you must justify everything you do in writing and you must be able to persuade a colleague. Three makes for good discussion. Each person, when you're only three, can express his or her views fully.

DOEBELE: And you discuss this verbally?

GINSBURG: Yes, oh yes. We discuss each one in turn until we are satisfied that three of us have said everything that we feel needs to be said about the case. It gets harder as the numbers increase. We will be sitting on Monday with eleven judges. If each one says in full everything that that judge wishes to say we may be in the conference room for hours. But three is a very good number for a discussion.

DOEBELE: I want to move into the issue of law schools and the education of the legal profession. You taught law at Rutgers and, as you said, Columbia. That was in the sixties and seventies, correct?

GINSBURG: Yes.

DOEBELE: What is your opinion of our current crop of law students coming up out of law schools across this country?

GINSBURG: They're very bright. They seem to get brighter all the time. My husband teaches at Georgetown and I go to law schools at least three times a year to give a lecture to judge a moot court argument. So, from what I can see, the law students are an able, enthusiastic group.

DOEBELE: What about the issue of the importance of coming from a Harvard or something like that? Do the names of those kinds of law schools still pull the weight, or can you go to a law school that maybe has less of a reputation and still move up as quickly?

GINSBURG: The law school's name will help in landing the first job. It becomes less important after that.

DOEBELE: One of the issues that Congress is currently talking about is a "litmus test" for judges, specifically the Senate Judiciary Committee taking a look at whether to accept the appointments of several federal judges. Do you have any feelings of what judges should go through before being accepted by the Senate?

GINSBURG: I think candidates for judgeships should not be asked questions about how they might decide a case that could come before them. If they give the answer to such a question then they can't sit on the case because they will have prejudged it. I think it would be absolutely wrong for Congress to inquire about issues in controversial cases that are coming before the courts to ask the judge, the candidate for the judgeship, how he or she would rule in that particular case.

DOEBELE: Well, you said you had been always interested in the issue of equal rights for men and women. Were those kinds of questions asked to you when you went before the Senate?

GINSBURG: There was an effort by a group to present those questions to me—a group of private citizens— and the committee did not allow those questions to be asked. Senator Metzenbaum was chairing at my hearing, Senator Dole was present at the hearing, and they considered those questions out of order.

DOEBELE: Do you have any aspirations for the Supreme Court?

GINSBURG: I'm entirely content with the job that I now have. But that is very challenging and just as I did not target the Court of Appeals for the D.C. Circuit as my life's ambition so I don't target any other job.

DOEBELE: A last question for you: One of the things we're doing in this series is talking about the mystery of the court. There seems to be an aura of mystery around the courts. People don't understand them, people may not understand how they can use them. And they certainly don't see them because of either television or whatever. What do you think about this? Should the judicial system be in this mysterious aura or is it? What is your opinion?

GINSBURG: I think it should not be. One of the great things about the United States is that our courts are open. Our proceedings are open to the public, both at the trial and the appellate level. Many times we have interesting cases and I stare out at an empty courtroom. I wish student groups, particularly high school student groups, even college groups in the area, would come and visit the court. I'm sure that we could arrange a program—our court, our chief executive, and the administrators from the schools. But there should be much more on both sides—on the side of the court and the side of community groups and schools—to increase understanding of what our courts are, how they can be used.

DOEBELE: Judge Ginsburg, thank you very much for being with us.

GINSBURG: It was a pleasure.

SUPREME COURT JUSTICE PERSPECTIVE

Q&A WITH STUDENTS FROM
MIDWOOD HIGH SCHOOL IN BROOKLYN,
NEW YORK, AND FROM MANCHESTER
HIGH SCHOOL IN MIDLOTHIAN, VIRGINIA
U.S. SUPREME COURT, EAST
CONFERENCE ROOM, WASHINGTON, D.C.
JANUARY 30, 2002

JUSTICE RUTH BADER GINSBURG: Be seated please. My very hearty welcome to the students from Midwood High School—the students of Midwood High School are on which side?—and the students from Manchester High School. And would you please identify yourselves, the Manchester students? So we have Midwood on this side and Manchester on that side.

I'll lead off with a few remarks about the Court's history, about our Constitution, and about life here at the Court. And then we will spend most of our time in conversation.

You've seen a bit of the Court. The building is very grand, don't you agree? This building became the Court's home in 1935, but the Court's history is far longer than that. The Court's history covers some 213 years and in that time, 108 justices have served on the bench of this court. Of that number, only two have been African American, and only two are women, but I expect those numbers will increase many times in the 21st century, not only in the judicial branch of our government but in the executive and the legislative branches as well. In all those branches, we are now beginning to draw on the talent of all of the people in this great nation. Do you know the opening words of our Constitution? Anyone volunteer. How does this Constitution begin? Yes?

STUDENT: We the people of the United States—

GINSBURG: We the people. We'll just stop there. We the people. Those are the opening words of the Constitution. But originally, those three words described a rather limited class. Who was left out? Well the Constitution was framed in 1787, and it specifically tolerated the slave trade until 1808, and even more than that, it required that if a slave should escape into a free state, the person who found the slave was bound to return him or her to his master. Women didn't become voters in this country until . . . who knows the year?

STUDENT: 1920.

GINSBURG: 1920, yes. So in the beginning, only white men who own property were truly part of "we the people." They were the only people who had the vote. But I think the great genius of our fundamental instrument of government is that in the course of its sometimes turbulent existence, this idea of "we the people" has grown to include people once left out, people once held in bondage, Native Americans, men who own no property, and thanks to the 19th amendment in 1920, women.

Every day, this court is visited by people from all around the USA and many foreign lands. Individual justices like me at this very moment meet with groups who come to see the Court. My favorite visit is school groups like yours. We've had students in the fourth grade, even in the second grade. But I think a high school audience profits best from the experience.

Let me tell you about a few nice customs that promote

friendship and respect among the nine justices. Before every court session and before every court conference, the justices come into the robing room and shake hands with each other before sitting down. And every day that we have arguments in court and every day that we confer, we also have lunch together in the justices' beautiful dining room which is on the second floor of this building, the floor that also includes my chambers. At the lunch table, we talk about anything and everything. It could be about the new exhibit at the National Gallery or the play that just opened at the Shakespeare Theater or the Washington Opera's latest spectacular production. And sometimes, we talk about our children and our grandchildren. We celebrate each others' birthdays with a lunchtime toast. And sometimes, for dessert, a cake baked by my husband, who is a super chef. My eldest granddaughter's third birthday was celebrated at a children's party in this very room. It was the first and I think still the only time that peanut butter and jelly sandwiches were the feature attraction on the buffet table. And beautiful wedding receptions have been held here for Justice Scalia's daughters and for Justice Kennedy's daughter.

Individually or in pairs—sometimes three and four justices—we visit law schools or we attend meetings with judges and with lawyers or community groups. It could be from as near as the District of Columbia or as far as Hawai'i. And some of us travel abroad in the Court's mid-winter recess or in the summer to teach or to learn about legal systems in faraway places like Europe, Israel, India, and Japan. To give you some recent examples, the chief justice and Justice Breyer this fall attended a meeting in Mexico with South and Central

American judges. Some weeks earlier, Justice O'Connor led a delegation of US judges to India. And Justice Kennedy periodically visits China as head of an American Bar Association commission.

Well, work at the court is very hard. But it is tremendously satisfying. The cases we decide are challenging. We will consider during our next sitting to take two stand-out examples: the question of whether it is constitutional to administer the death penalty to a person who is mentally retarded. We will also hear arguments in February on whether a state may give the parents of school children vouchers that cover parochial school tuition. We are constantly reading, thinking, and trying to write so that lawyers and other judges will understand our rulings. Sometimes I still wake up wondering whether it was all a beautiful dream. It is, being a Supreme Court justice, the best job in the world for a lawyer, I believe. Well, I think I talked my allotted time, so now I'll be very glad to have this conversation that is your reason for being here. And I think we can take a question from Manchester and then from Midwood. We'll do it in alphabetical order so Manchester will go first. Who has a question? Yes, in the second row.

STUDENT: My name is Jaime Bates, and I'm a senior at Manchester High School. How do you think the Virginia Military Institute decision, making it coed, has affected the overall struggle for women's rights?

GINSBURG: The Virginia Military Institute case, for those of you who don't know what that was about, it was about a school maintained by the state in Virginia that gave a good education and a continuing interest in students becoming sometimes military leaders—that was not the most common pattern—business and community leaders. It was a grand opportunity but the state afforded it only to members of one sex. And the Virginia Military Institute some years ago opened its doors to women—I think they've already had their first women graduates.

It was one of a series of cases in which doors that were tightly closed—not so long ago—were open. You may not know that it wasn't until the end of the 1970s that in every state in the union, women began to serve on juries on the same basis as men. And there were many occupations thought improper for women. Well, the Virginia Military Institute case is one of a line of decisions—some of them by this court and some by other courts, some by legislatures without any court intervention—saying that no doors should be closed to people who have the talent and the will to enter and do the job. Did that answer your question? Let's have one from Madison. In the second row, yes?

STUDENT: Hello, good afternoon Justice Ginsburg—

GINSBURG: I'm sorry, you must excuse me. I must interject that I'm from Madison High in Brooklyn and you're from Midwood. You were our rivals then; I don't know if that's still the case.

STUDENT: We beat you this football season, sorry. [*Laughs*] My name is Lucia Franklin and I'm junior president at Midwood

High School. I was wondering, through your experiences as a woman in the law profession and being the second female justice out of 108 justices in the Supreme Court, do you feel that it's harder for women to be recognized or even to be taken seriously as part of the government?

GINSBURG: The answer is yes, but less hard than it was a generation ago, and it will be less hard for my daughter's generation, her daughter's generation. As more women are out there doing things, other women are encouraged by it and I think that we're all better off for it. As I said in my opening remarks, this nation benefits enormously from using the talent of all of its people to do the hard thinking and the heavy work that's needed to move us forward. Let's take the back row, yes?

STUDENT: Hi Justice Ginsburg. My name is Kristin Guilfers, and I'm a sophomore at the Mass Communications Center at Manchester High School and I was just wondering, in all of history, who, in your opinion has been the best president and why?

GINSBURG: I would have to say Abraham Lincoln because he kept us one nation and because he wrote and spoke so beautifully. He was truly a man who wrote the way some artists paint. There are many other great presidents, but Lincoln, in my view, was the finest. Let's take the third row, yes?

STUDENT: Good afternoon Justice Ginsburg. You're one of the 108 who have the great chance to serve in the Supreme

Court and I was just wondering who was your mentor or who is your mentor, and who would you choose to have inspired you to become a justice in the Supreme Court?

GINSBURG: I can't say that I had a mentor or a role model for becoming any kind of a judge because when I graduated from law school, women just were not on the bench. The first woman ever appointed to a federal court judgeship was appointed in 1934 by President Franklin Delano Roosevelt. And when I graduated from law school there were no women on a federal court of appeals. Then President Johnson appointed another in 1968, but women were what I called one-at-a-time curiosities. So, no woman law graduate of my era aspired to become any kind of judge. She hoped that she would be able to make a living as a lawyer.

It wasn't until President Jimmy Carter's time in office that both women and members of minority groups showed up on the bench in numbers. And to President Carter's great credit that was not haphazard—there was no accident. He deliberately set about to change the face—to change the complexion—of the US judiciary so that it would genuinely reflect all of the nation's people—all of the talent in this nation and not just part of it. So, when Jimmy Carter became president, he took the only then-federal appellate judge who was a woman, and made her his first Secretary of Education. And then there were none. He quickly appointed 25 [women] to federal courts of appeals across the country and many more to sit on trial benches. And after Jimmy Carter's precedent-setting move, that became the pattern. And every president recognized the value of drawing on the talent of orderly people. And, too, President Reagan deserves the great credit of appointing the first woman to this court. We're ready for one from Manchester now. In the back row, yes.

STUDENT: Hello, Justice Ginsburg. I'm Carrie Collins, and I'm a freshman at the Mass Communications Center at Manchester High School. I was wondering what inspired you to pursue a career in law?

GINSBURG: Well, a few things. One is—I will confess that if I could have any talent God could give me, I would be a great diva because I simply love opera. But the problem is I am a monotone. In my grade school, P.S. 238, I was put in with the—they were called sparrows as opposed to the robins, and I was told to mouth the words. So being a great diva was not in the cards for me.

I liked to think and to talk and to persuade both in writing and orally. And law seemed to be a field where those skills would come in handy. But there was a problem: would there be a job for me? I was encouraged by one of my professors at Cornell University. He was a man who taught government. His name was Robert E. Kushman. And I went to college in a time that was not such a good one for the United States. It's today known as the McCarthy era, when many people were afraid to speak their minds because it might be considered un-American to disagree with the government's policies. This professor made me conscious of what was going on in our country and also conscious that brave lawyers were standing up and speaking out against the kind of overbearing questions from the Senate and the House that were truly un-American.

And so, this great teacher gave me the courage to believe that I could become a lawyer and that lawyers could do some good for their community and their country. That and my husband. We went to law school together and he is a person who was so confident in his own ability that he never regarded me as any kind of threat. He has always been my biggest booster. Now there were many other people that made it possible for me, including a wonderful mother-in-law, but I think the two who waited [on] me most [were] that wonderful teacher and my life's companion. Now we are on the Midwood side. Let's take in the third row, yes?

STUDENT: Hi Justice Ginsburg, good afternoon. My name is Hattie Lotta, and I'm from Midwood High School and I'm a senior. My question is the following: if you could serve as Supreme Court justice in any past case before your appointment, which one would it be and why?

GINSBURG: Which past case? Well, it might be one that this great Chief Justice Marshall decided. [*Points to portrait behind her*] It has the name *Marbury v. Madison* and it established the principle that the Constitution–this Constitution is not just an aspirational document, it is the law of the land, the highest law to be applied by the judges in cases in which it is relevant. That notion of judicial review for constitutionality was not practiced elsewhere in the world. It was a great precedent that was set in that case and that has steered the course of the US judiciary through the ages. Yes?

STUDENT: Hi, my name is Amanda Tuck. I'm a senior at

Manchester High School and I was wondering, do you think that allowing recording devices and other forms of broadcast media in the courtroom would negatively affect the outcome of a case?

GINSBURG: I don't think it would affect the outcome of the case, but I do think that there are problems with it. And the principal problem is who is in control of the proceeding? Now, if it's going to be a gavel to gavel show as I understand New York's highest court has, there will be a problem for the producers of the show because watching the court argument from start to finish can sometimes be rather tedious. On the other hand, if someone is cutting it—taking a snippet from here and a snippet from there, they can give an altogether false impression.

One concern is that lawyers tend to act up for the camera in a way that they would not if they were giving a presentation just to the bench and the people in the courtroom. Another is that a judge might be concerned about phrasing a particular question, a question that would be well understood in a conversation among law-trained people, but that might not play too well on the television. So, I don't think it would have any effect on the outcome of cases, but I'm glad that some of the courts are experimenting with the use of cameras, so then we'll have a body of experience to rely on in deciding what should be the next step. Yes, in the second row.

STUDENT: Hi my name is Gillian, I'm a senior at Midwood High School, and I wanted to know in making your decision after hearing a case, do you first consider justice or legal procedure and does that affect the way that you select a case that you'd like to hear.

GINSBURG: Do I first consider justice or legal procedure? I hope those two are not on different tracks because judicial procedure is all about a fair and orderly presentation of a case. So we on this court very much respect what's called "precedent" and what that means is decisions that were written earlier become precedent for another case. The reason for that is [that] we need some stability in the system. If every case is gonna be a new thing, the rules of the game will change today from what they were yesterday and no one will know how to go about his or her business, so precedent is important for that reason. Justice is of course an ingredient in law making. What does it say over the portals of this court as you entered? Did you come in by the main entrance or the side? Yes? [*Student responds quietly.*] Equal justice under law, yes. So that is the ideal, and law should be developed to serve justice. Let's see, in the third row.

STUDENT: Good afternoon. I'm Erica Wells, I'm a sophomore at Manchester High School. During the early part of your career, you had difficulty with equal opportunities because you're a woman. Does that make you partial to cases that come before you involving minorities?

GINSBURG: Does it make me partial? I think people who have been a minority in some respect in their lives will be sensitive to what it's like to be outside the dominant group. That doesn't mean that someone who is in the dominant group can't also be very sensitive, but there is something about having yourself been in a position of being not really wanted that makes you sympathetic to other people who are in that position. Let's take this second row in the middle, yes?

STUDENT: Good afternoon Justice Ginsburg. My name is Deirdre Holder and I'm a junior at Midwood High School. I just wanted to know what has the experience of being a female associate justice in the Supreme Court been like for you? Is it what you expected?

GINSBURG: Is being a justice what I expected? Pretty much so because this court is not entirely new to me. I was a lawyer arguing cases here in the 1970s and then I worked for thirteen years just three or four blocks down the road at the US Courthouse on Constitution Avenue, so I knew what this court does. Oh, I was also a law teacher for some seventeen years and one of the subjects I taught was civil procedure and another subject that I taught was constitutional law.

What has changed for me most and what I had not encountered before was the tremendous publicity that goes with being one of only nine. When I was a federal court appeals judge, I was one of a hundred-odd. Being one of only nine means that you are noticed in some ways. In some ways that's very nice and in other ways that could be, oh, mildly annoying. For example, the nice part: I remember going to Macy's in Pentagon City soon after I was appointed to the bench. And salespeople came flocking to me to ask if they could help. Before that it was very hard to find someone who would assist me. What's not so nice about being watched is, well, for example: my first year one of the papers reported that I'm so compulsive about doing my work that I was seen at movie previews opening my mail. So you don't want to have the sense that when you're doing private things someone is looking over your shoulder, but it's a small price, that intrusion on your privacy, to the tremendous satisfactions that this job holds.

STUDENT: Good afternoon, Justice Ginsburg. My name is Emily Wingo, and I'm a sophomore at Manchester High School at the Mass Communications Center and I just wanted to know, what are your thoughts on Napster?

GINSBURG: Well, I can give you my thoughts on Napster. The stock answer is Napster presents an issue that may very well come before us at the court and, therefore, I don't want to preview my views.

This court, you probably know, is a reactive institution, that is, it doesn't initiate things the way Congress does or the president does. It waits for people to request the Court to take a case and then briefs are filed. Now those are lawyers' endeavors to tell us what a case is about or what they think the law requires. The word brief is a misnomer because briefs are seldom if ever brief. On this court it's fifty pages aside just for the opening brief.

In any case, when and if we should get to a case like Napster, we will be informed not only by the lawyers' briefs but by many decisions in other federal courts. This court, you know, is the final instance, but not the first instance. We will have decisions from trial courts, from courts of appeals on that issue. We will have many people filing friend of the court briefs. So when I appear on the bench to listen to an argument, I've done a lot of homework and it's all things that the parties or interested members of the public have presented to me. I make a judgement not on the basis of my own private proclivities or even on the basis of my own private research, but on the basis of what has been presented by the many people who are interested in that decision. So I don't try to preview my views, one, because that would be inappropriate, another, because I'm not informed yet, the way that I will be. The question you asked is a good one for my daughter because she's also in the law business. She's a law teacher at Columbia Law School and her field is literary property, so she knows all about the Napster case, and I may [know about Napster] on the day that that case or another like it is argued before this court. Now we're up to Midwood again. Yes?

STUDENT: Hello Justice Ginsburg. My name is Karen Tseng, and I'm a junior at Midwood High School. In the [inaudible] case, you believed that the Fifth Amendment is very important. Has your opinion changed after the September 11th events? Why or why not?

GINSBURG: In the which case?

STUDENT: In the [inaudible] case.* It was argued in 1998. It was about a foreign immigrant having, writing false information on an immigration form application.

* Probably *United States v. Balsys*.

GINSBURG: This was in the court of appeals or the Supreme Court?

STUDENT: In the Supreme Court.

GINSBURG: Well, my view of the Fifth Amendment surely has not changed. You're talking about one piece of the Fifth Amendment. The Fifth Amendment says many things including the right to be indicted by a grand jury and perhaps the most famous clause is not the one you have in mind, but it's "nor shall any person be deprived of life, liberty, or property without due process of law." The Fifth Amendment also provides that private property shall not be taken for public use without just compensation and protection against double jeopardy. But I suppose what you're referring to is that "no person shall be held to answer for a crime," well that's the grand jury. You are probably thinking of what's called the self-incrimination clause, that "nor shall any person be compelled in any criminal case to be a witness against himself." That, I think, is fundamental to the way we do justice, that is, the prosecutor must prove a person guilty, the person is not tortured to confess as the way some countries still do their decision-making. No one rubs salt into the defendant's eye, but it is the burden of the prosecutor to prove not only that it's more likely than not that the defendant committed the crime but what is the standard that's used—what are juries told? To convict you must find . . . yes?

STUDENT: Beyond a reasonable doubt?

GINSBURG: Beyond a reasonable doubt. And it is the prosecutor's burden. You know, any time when there is a stressful
situation, our reaction might be: "Well, our security comes
first. We don't care about our freedom." Of course we're concerned about our security, but if we gave up our freedom
as the price for security, we would no longer be the great
nation that we are. So everything in the Fifth Amendment
is important to me, more so, if anything, since September
11th than before, because the job that we have is to show the
world what are the values of our country and why our country could never be put down by an episode like that. That our
true strength comes from being a land of freedom, a land of
liberty, a land of democracy. And now up to, let's see, in the
second row, yes?

STUDENT: My name is William Collins and I'm a senior at
Manchester High School. I'd like to go back to something
you were talking about earlier with precedents. In my government class, my teacher, Delegate Cox, has said that sometimes in the past, justices have gone against what they believe
or felt was right so that they didn't have to overturn prece-
dence. Have you ever come across a situation like this and if
you have what have you done?

GINSBURG: There was a great justice of this court, Justice
Brandeis, who said "some cases are better decided than decided right." What he meant by that is: in some instances—
particularly when we're talking about not a great clause of the
Constitution but a provision in one of the dense statutes that
Congress produces—what's important is that people know
what the law is so that they can conduct their conduct in

accordance with that law. And in such cases, one might well defer to the majority view because what's important is that there be a rule of the road, and it could be one thing or it could be another thing. But we should all agree on what it is. So it depends on the kind of case that we're talking about. And in cases that involve what does a particular statute mean—where if the court gets it wrong and the legislature thinks that the answer should be something other than what the court gave, the legislature can fix it. So there are many cases where I think judges will say, "well, if I were king or if I were queen I would rule this way, but since a clear majority goes the other way, I will add my vote to give the decision even more weight."

Now if it's a fundamental question, it isn't one's personal view. If judges were to engage in just pressing their personal view unaided by history and prior decisions, if they were to do that, then we'd have pandemonium. And I think what restrains all of us—here we are nine and if we were each to say, "I'm going to rule on every case the way I would if I were the king," then we would have no cohesive decisions. We would have chaos. And so all of us are mindful that we're sitting on a collegial court and we're not here to press what we may regard as our own superior wisdom, but to rule in the light of history and law and legal decisions and as a member of this honorable court.

Yes, second row?

STUDENT: Hi, my name is Krystle Ford and I'm a senior and also the mayor of Midwood High School. Justice Ginsburg, as a woman, you know, there may be sometimes when your mercy comes into your judgement. How are you as a judge just and merciful at the same time?

GINSBURG: Well, I hope that I am as a human because I know many men who would agree with Shakespeare that the quality of mercy is not strained. Now, as I said, that is a part of judging. It is not the only ingredient. The empathy that one feels for another human, I said in answer to a question that was asked before: if you've been in the position of being the victim of discrimination you may be more sensitive to other people who were in that situation. But I must say, I wouldn't ascribe my feeling of empathy simply to being a woman. If you came to my chambers, you would see a photograph of my first grandchild with his father, my son-in-law, and the love that's communicated between those two humans is simply beautiful and I've thought many times how much better our world would be if men felt themselves free to show that they are filled with human caring and that they can relate to children with as much love as women do. Let's see, I want to pick people who haven't spoken before, so, I think you haven't. Yes?

STUDENT: Good afternoon, I'm Jillian Nardufus from the Mass Communications Center at Manchester High School. Justice Ginsburg, have you ever experienced a case where your political views were not congruent with your interpretation of the Constitution?

GINSBURG: I would answer that question: yes, and in the same way that I've answered other questions, I'm not here to be the political leader. That I am here to help interpret and enforce not simply the Constitution but all of the federal laws, and so yes, there are cases where I would never have voted for whatever is the law that Congress just passed, but it is the law and so I have to apply it—construe it as fairly and reasonably as I can—and apply it. Second row, yes?

STUDENT: My name is Keith Ledger, I'm a senior at Midwood High School, and I was wondering: has there ever been a case in which you made your own opinion and then changed your opinion based on what the other judges had to say, and why?

GINSBURG: Yes, and there have been many, not only in my years here, but when I was on a court of appeals where we generally sat three judges on a panel. Yes, you listen to your colleagues. All of us are skilled in the art of persuasion and we do it in many ways: in the memos we write to each other, in the conversations we have—formally at our conferences, informally by telephone, in the halls. We're constantly trying to persuade each other. And I have been persuaded by my colleagues' views as I hope my colleagues have by mine on some occasions.

Yes, this is a collegial business and I might tell you that as much as the press tends to emphasize the divisions on this court—the 5–4 decisions—we are unanimous in our judgements in about 40 percent of the cases we decide. And considering that we don't take cases generally, unless other courts have disagreed on what the right answer is, that's a pretty good record of unanimity, 40 percent. That compares to about 25 percent where we will divide 5–4, but more often we are able to unanimously agree on a single decision or at least a single judgement and that's because we do listen to each other. But the collegial process, that's what it's all about—expressing your views, hoping to be persuasive yourself and recognizing when someone else's argument is persuasive.

In the second row, yes?

STUDENT: Yes, Justice Ginsburg, my name is Stephen Kierekidas. I'm a senior at Manchester High School. I just want to know: in your years on all the courts, not just the Supreme Court, has there ever been a controversial case or circumstance that has made you regret your decision to go into this profession?

GINSBURG: Well, let me tell you some very good advice that I got from a colleague when I was on the court of appeals. He was a fine judge, his name was Ed Tanner, and he said, "Do the very best job you can in each case, but when it's done and when the opinion is released, don't look back, don't worry over past decisions. Go on to the next case and give it your all." And so I have followed that advice and it has served me very well.

Yes, in the next-to-last row?

STUDENT: Good afternoon, Justice Ginsburg. I'm Greg Staminas, a senior at Midwood High School, and I was just wondering what your opinion was of President Bush's State of the Union address last evening?

GINSBURG: The part that I heard was very effective, and what seemed to me quite telling was that when Gephardt made his response, so much of it was in agreement of the need to work together in a bipartisan way in dealing with this new challenge that we have. Now I didn't hear all of it because I left the court late last night, but I turned on the radio and I heard a good part of it.

Let's see, on this side who has not—? You haven't, all right.

STUDENT: Good afternoon, Justice Ginsburg. My name is Ashley Cheney and I'm a sophomore at Manchester High School in the Mass Communications Center. Earlier, you were talking about how you loved to meet with high school students, and I was wondering if you would give one piece of advice to high school students, what would it be and why?

GINSBURG: It would be to follow your dream. Believe that, as I said before, no doors are closed if you genuinely have the will to do it. And that whatever you choose to do, leave tracks, and that means: don't do just for yourself because in the end it's not going to be fully satisfying. I think you will want to leave the world a little better for your having lived. And there's no satisfaction a person can gain from just from what people call turning over a buck that's equal to the satisfaction that you get from knowing that you have made another's life, your community a little better for your effort.

I have a ten-minute sign, so we want to take only people who a haven't asked questions yet, so . . . You have not?

STUDENT: [inaudible] ma'am. I'm of Midwood High School in the 12th grade. What can the government do to further democratize this country to correct the uneven distribution of power in the country and improve the people's understanding of government and make the government more democratic?

GINSBURG: Well you can recognize that we are far from perfect, but when I started the talk, I said to you, do you know what "we the people" meant in 1787? Our whole history has been for including more and more people, giving more and more people a say in the government, and so far we have succeeded rather well in that effort. I expect that we will continue along that course. Yes?

STUDENT: Hi, I'm Ashley Muscleman. I'm from Manchester High School and I'm a senior. And I'm just wondering, are there any cases that you believe should have come before the Supreme Court but didn't necessarily get the four judges' vote to come before the court?

GINSBURG: The question is: do I think there should have been cases to come here that didn't. My answer is, if they should have they probably will. Let me explain to you a bit about how we work: we have now over 8,000 petitions for review a year. Of those, we select for decisions less than 100—somewhere between 70 and 90. How do we select them? It will take four votes to grant a petition for rebuke. And if a petition attracts fewer than four votes, the petition will be denied automatically. This court takes cases when other courts are divided about what the law is—whether constitutional law [or] statutory law. If a case is causing that kind of disagreement in lower courts, that issue will come up again and again. So I think if I've made mistakes, it's been sometimes in granting a case that should not have been granted, either because it was too soon or because the facts weren't right. If we deny review and the issue is really important, we will have many opportunities to take that question later. So I don't worry over my votes to deny.

I have been told that the rules are that I should allow questions only from the students, so I will follow that. So you have asked a question. You have also? Is there someone on the Midwood side who would like to ask a question who hasn't yet? . . . All right, then we'll take your repeat question.

STUDENT: Hello, again. It's Anna from Midwood High School and I'm a senior. I'm on the school newspaper and I was wondering: for those young ladies at our school who wish to become lawyers and maybe someday take your seat or another seat on the panel of the nine justices, what advice do you have or maybe a word of caution for those who wish to become lawyers? Thank you.

GINSBURG: Become a well-educated person. People who are pre-law sometimes say, well should I major in government? And my answer is major in whatever you like: music, art. Become a well-educated person, someone who appreciates good literature, who knows a little bit about philosophy. The law—and I'm very fond of lawyers—the law is a learned profession and it isn't like being expert in a craft, like being a baker or a shoemaker. Very important jobs, but law is a true profession—and it's a learned profession. And so you're not just preparing a will for someone or writing a corporate charter. You are being a counselor and to be a wise counselor you should be a well-educated, well-read person.

This should be our last question, I think, on Manchester side. Have you asked a question before? Fine, then please do.

STUDENT: Hi, I'm Nikki Vector from Manchester High School and I'm a 12th grader. My question to you is: in the past you have stated your feelings on the litmus tests and I was wondering what alterations, if any, would you have that you would like to see for the nominations of justices and judges?

GINSBURG: Federal judges are appointed for life and I don't think that there is anything wrong—in fact I think that there is a plus—that for the moment of the appointment, that moment in time before you were going to get a job that you keep for life, that you be exposed to the political branches. The president selects and then the Senate confirms. For one thing, for the rest of your life as a judge you'll be sitting in a high place asking questions. It makes you more empathetic if you have been on the receiving end of questions, say from the Senate Judiciary Committee.

I think that the question should be to try to determine, does this person have the knowledge, does this person have the sympathetic understanding to be a good judge, and it should not be about how will she vote in a particular case. Presidents who try to pick judges on that basis sometimes are sorely disappointed, because you do have that freedom to decide without worrying about if you are going to lose the job, will Congress cut your pay, because the Constitution said they can't do that either.

What I think might be improved, at least for the nominations of Supreme Court justices, is to consolidate the proceeding. Mine went on for a week and it was not necessary. One or two days would have been adequate. I tend to think it stretched out that far because it was an opportunity for the senators to appear before the camera. But I do think it is healthy to have that moment when the judge is being confronted and as long as the questions are about the judge's knowledge, the judge's understanding, and not about how would you vote on this or that case, it's all right.

How are we doing on time? Yes? Do we have a last question?

STUDENT: Good afternoon once again. You said earlier that when you were younger you would have liked to have been a diva. Now after all these years and your experiences in government in your career, would you trade it all in to be a diva?

GINSBURG: That's a powerfully hard question. Well, perhaps if I could retain my voice as long as say, Placido Domingo, who's singing beautifully into his sixties, but there is something about a lawyer's job that is superior to a diva's job and that is: we can write and we can think and we can read—aided by glasses after a certain age—but we can do that into our 70s, 80s, and some even into their 90s, and I don't think that any singer can manage that. So as I grow older, I begin to think that maybe it's better to be a lawyer or a judge. [*Applause*]

45 WORDS: A CONVERSATION ABOUT THE FIRST AMENDMENT WITH SUPREME COURT JUSTICES ANTONIN SCALIA AND RUTH BADER GINSBURG

INTERVIEW BY MARVIN KALB

THE KALB REPORT

THE NATIONAL PRESS CLUB, WASHINGTON, D.C.

APRIL 17, 2014

MARVIN KALB: Hello, and welcome to the National Press Club and to another edition of the Kalb Report. I'm Marvin Kalb and our program tonight: "45 Words: A Conversation about the First Amendment with Supreme Court Justices Antonin Scalia and Ruth Bader Ginsburg." It would be an honor, obviously, to have one Supreme Court justice as my guest, but to have two is indeed a very special privilege, especially these two, who generally represent contrasting opinions on the Court—one liberal, the other conservative—and yet they are great friends who dine together, travel together, love going to the opera together. In fact, they inspired a new opera called, of all things, "Scalia/Ginsburg." [*Laughter*] They are like the old days in this Capitol when political differences would not stop a good friendship from flourishing.

Justice Scalia is the longest-serving justice on today's Supreme Court, appointed by President Ronald Reagan in 1986. He's called an originalist, meaning he believes that the Constitution ought to be interpreted more or less as the Founding Fathers meant for it to be interpreted. "You want change," he says, "change the legislature; change the law." His job is to interpret the law.

Justice Ginsburg was appointed to the Supreme Court by President Bill Clinton in 1993. Her view is that the

Constitution is what has been called a "living" document, meaning it changes as society changes, one linked to the other. Tradition and precedent matter, of course, but they do not necessarily determine her legal judgment.

Both justices, despite this difference between them, have devoted their lives to the law, to teaching, to democracy and to freedom. We're going to discuss freedom of the press, but let's start with what the concept of freedom means—its origin, its meaning at the time of the American Revolution and its meaning in today's America. I've always been fascinated by the fact that the first commandment of the Ten Commandments in the Bible and the First Amendment in the Constitution both stress the central importance of freedom; the first commandment saying, "I am the Lord thy God, who brought thee forth out of Egypt, out of the house of bondage, and thou shalt have no other god before me." Out of bondage to what, if not freedom? The First Amendment guarantees us freedom of religion, of speech or of the press, of the right peaceably to assemble, to petition our government for a redress of grievances.

Justice Scalia, in your view, is there a link between the first commandment and the First Amendment? Did one possibly inspire the other?

JUSTICE ANTONIN SCALIA: Oh, I doubt it. [*Laughter*]

KALB: Ok.

SCALIA: I think our Constitution was inspired by the traditions of the common law. And I think what our framers meant by the freedom of speech, for example, was that freedom of speech which was the birthright of Englishmen at the time. I don't think it has anything to do with Moses. [*Laughter*]

I think what freedom meant at the time was the absence of constraint, the absence of coercion. So freedom of religion, for example, meant that you could not be constrained to contribute to the support of a church that you didn't believe in, you could not be disabled from holding certain public offices because of your religion—the absence of coercion. And I think it was the same for freedom of speech.

KALB: And, Justice Ginsburg, your view.

JUSTICE RUTH BADER GINSBURG: Marvin, this is the one question you told us you might ask us. I was puzzled by it because as I read the Ten Commandments, the first four of them are not about freedom; they're about humans' obligations to God. So, thou shalt have no other god before me, no graven images, keep the Sabbath holy—everything obligations that people owe to the Almighty. But I also mentioned to you that your question comes at just the right season because this is the Passover, and the Passover is indeed a celebration of the liberation of a people. And there are many words in the Haggadah that celebrate freedom. So I would take the Passover service, rather than the stern first four commandments, as advancing the idea of freedom.

KALB: Well, I knew I'd be wrong, but—[*Laughter*]—I mean, I knew that to start with, but—

SCALIA: You thought you'd be wrong on the law, not on theology. [*Laughter*]

KALB: No, but what I would like to get at is really what your sense is that the people who wrote the Constitution had in their minds when they talked about freedom. Now, you mentioned common law. Common law was not explicit about freedom. Many different interpretations were there. And what I'm trying to get at is before we get into the specifics of freedom of the press, I would like to know what the concept meant in your understanding.

SCALIA: Oh, I don't think the common law was that diverse as far as what every aspect of freedom consisted of. The freedom of speech, for example, it was very clear that that did not include the freedom to libel, that you could be subject to a lawsuit for libel. And that type of coercion was not considered incompatible with the freedom of speech. Now, some aspects of it I suppose were more vague, but some things were pretty clear.

KALB: And, Justice Ginsburg, the concept of freedom is very prominently featured in the Constitution. It's right there in the First Amendment. And the writer Tom Paine had a simple explanation. He wrote, "It would be strange indeed if so celestial an article as freedom should not be highly rated."

So it does seem to me—and I'll get back to this again and again, I think—that if you're going to feature the concept of freedom right up there at the top, you have to have had something in your head about the importance of freedom to what it is that you were doing at that time, which was beginning to build a democracy.

GINSBURG: There's a point Justice Scalia made in his opening remarks. He said he sees this First Amendment as protection against constraint, government constraint. And there I think our expression of the First Amendment is quite different from, for example, the expression in the Declaration of the Rights of Man, the great French document. This First Amendment is saying: Hands off, government. It doesn't say everyone shall have the right to speak freely. That's what the Declaration of the Rights of Man says, everyone shall have the right to speak freely. Not at all. This says Congress shall make no law abridging the freedom of speech or of the press. So it's directed to government and it says: Government, hands off. These rights already exist and you must not touch them.

KALB: John Stuart Mill, the—I'm sorry. Please.

SCALIA: I was going to—it should not be painted as the foundation of the American democracy, this concept of freedom. Don't forget that the Bill of Rights was an afterthought. It was not what they debated about in Philadelphia in 1787. Now, a couple of the states that ratified the Constitution made it clear that they expected there to be a bill of rights added, but it was added in 1791 on the proposal of the First Congress.

What they thought would preserve a free society was the structure of the government. That's what they debated about in 1787. And if you think that's false, just look around the world. Every tinhorn dictator in the world today has a bill of rights. It isn't a bill of rights that produces freedom. It's the structure of government that prevents anybody from seizing all the power. Once that happens, you ignore the bill of rights. So, you know, keep your eye on the ball. Structure is destiny.

KALB: The eye on the ball being to keep your eye on the structure of the government.

SCALIA: Well, our structure is so different from that of most of the world. There are very few countries, for example, that have a bicameral legislature, a genuine one, including England. They don't have a real bicameral. The House of Lords can't do anything. [*Laughter*] Well, they can make the Commons pass the bill a second time. And when they pass it a second time it becomes law.

There are very few countries, none of the parliamentary countries, that have a separately elected president. The chief executive, in all the countries of Europe, is the tool of the parliament. There's never any serious disagreement between them. When there is, they kick them out. They have a no-confidence vote and have an election and appoint a new tool. I mean, we are so different from the rest of the world, and it is that that has, more than anything else, preserved our liberties. And you wouldn't want to live in most of the countries of the world that have a bill of rights which guarantees freedom of speech and of the press. You wouldn't want to live there.

GINSBURG: I have to disagree with my colleague in that respect.

KALB: I'm glad that you can do it. I can't. [*Laughter*]

GINSBURG: First, I don't think that the rest of the world is regarding our legislature at the current moment as a model to be followed. [*Laughter, applause*] And, second, however it was understood in the beginning, yes, the structure of government was to protect our liberties, but there was always the idea of rights. Think of our first great document, the Declaration of Independence.

Also, it is true that the great protections that the press now has came rather late. The First Amendment was developed in a serious way—around the time of the First World War it began. So the freedom that's enjoyed today, the freedom to speak and to write, was not a big-ticket item in the Supreme Court until rather late.

SCALIA: Well, it was a big-ticket item mostly because until the middle of the 20th century—believe it, the middle of the 20th century—it was not thought that the Bill of Rights applied to the states. It was only a limitation on what the federal government could do, not a limitation on what the states could do. That was—that's why we never had, you know, until the middle of the 20th century these cases about whether you can have a crèche in the—in the city square. Is it OK if you have a menorah next to it, maybe Santa Claus on top? [*Laughter*] I mean, we didn't have any of those silly cases. It was only when the Bill of Rights was imposed upon the states that we began to have them. And so a lot of the restrictions on speech that—you know, that would be imposed by states would not have been thought to violate our Bill of Rights— maybe the states' bill of rights but not ours.

KALB: But I'm wondering, at the time that the structure of government was set up close to two hundred years ago, what is it that the Founding Fathers had in mind when they thought about freedom? And one definition advanced by John Stuart Mill I found very compelling, but I don't know whether that's what they had in mind. He spoke about "absolute freedom of opinion and sentiment on all subjects practical or speculative, scientific, moral or theological." And I'm wondering if that is what Madison, Monroe had in mind at that time or whether they had a more narrow vision of freedom. Justice Ginsburg?

GINSBURG: I wouldn't call the vision narrow, but there are no absolute rights, even though if you read the First Amendment it does sound that way. It says, "Congress shall pass no law."

KALB: No law.

GINSBURG: But of course there are laws that Congress can pass. So the idea of an absolute right, I don't know any right that doesn't have limitations.

KALB: Even at that time, in the minds of the Founding Fathers?

GINSBURG: Yes, I think so.

KALB: Explain why in the First Amendment, after listing the phrase "freedom of speech," the Founding Fathers found it necessary, or wanted to add, four crucially important words: or of the press. Freedom of the press is what they were talking about, but why did they add that phrase? Why was it necessary? Justice Scalia?

SCALIA: I think it's a natural addition. All it means is the freedom to speak and to write. It wasn't referring to the institutional press, to guys that run around in a fedora hat with a sticker in it that says "press." I'm not sure that they even referred to the [*mimes quotation marks*] "institutional press" in those days. It meant the freedom to speak and to publish. And that, that clause has been interpreted not to give any special prerogatives to the institutional press. It gives prerogatives to anybody who has a Xerox machine.

KALB: What do you mean "institutional press," forgive me? What does that mean?

SCALIA: I mean those organizations whose business is writing and publishing. NBC, CBS, you.

KALB: I like that! [*Laughter*]

GINSBURG: One idea that we didn't take from England was the office of the censor, who censored books before they were published. And that I think was part of putting in this protection of the press and we have never had in the United States government an office of the censor, which plagued people in England and on the continent. Think of Verdi and having to put his opera plots—

SCALIA: Oh, you have to bring opera into it, don't you. I knew you were going to do that. [*Laughter*]

KALB: Was it understood that there were limitations on the press back then? Was it understood, that there were limitations?

SCALIA: Well, yes, on speech and on oral speech and written speech, both. I told you, libel laws. Libel laws were one thing.

KALB: Yes, but what about the press at that time. What were they thinking about at that time?

SCALIA: I don't know that there were any special rules applicable to the press. The press did not have to get permission of a censor to publish, but neither did anybody else.

GINSBURG: And the press annoyed some very important figures in our history, like Thomas Jefferson.

KALB: Yes indeed, and it's interesting that Jefferson before he became president spoke very highly of the press, but while he was president, spoke about it as a polluted area and you couldn't believe a thing in any newspaper.

GINSBURG: But how it's survived, one thing that epitomizes for me the importance of freedom of speech is in the ballot for America: the right to speak my mind out. That's America, to me.

SCALIA: Now I think if you had to pick, and you probably shouldn't have to, but if you had to pick one freedom that is the most essential to the functioning of a democracy, it has to be freedom of speech. Because democracy means persuading one another and then ultimately voting and the majority rules. You can't run such a system if there is muzzling of one point of view. So it's a fundamental freedom in a democracy—much more necessary in a democracy than in any other system of government. I guess you can run an effective monarchy without freedom of speech. I don't think you can run an effective democracy without it.

KALB: But on this matter of press freedom, John Adams wrote that "Mankind cannot now be governed without it, nor it present with it." And it seems that the idea of a free press has always been a problem for a succession of American presidents, but in a broader sense, do you feel we could have endured as a democracy from then to now without a free press. What do you think, Justice Ginsburg?

GINSBURG: I don't think so. I think the press has played a tremendously important role as watchdog over what the government is doing, and that keeps the government from getting too far out of line, because they will be in the limelight. So yes, there are all kinds of excesses in the press too, but we have to put up with that, I think, given the alternative.

KALB: Justice Scalia, you want to comment on that issue?

SCALIA: No, I agree with that, of course.

GINSBURG: It's hard to keep the freedom of the press, because there are many people who don't like what the press is publishing. There was a cartoon just after the Revolutionary War, and it shows a Tory being carted off by the police and the caption is: "Liberty of speech to those who speak the speech of liberty." So the right to speak against government, against what is the prevailing of view of society, is tremendously important.

SCALIA: Including the right to speak against democracy, I mean don't forget that. Some of the biggest fights were whether free speech includes freedom to speak against freedom of speech or against democracy. And it's plausible that it doesn't, but of course, we have rejected that view. Communists were entitled to say this democratic system doesn't work, let's get rid of it.

GINSBURG: That took awhile for that idea to take hold because there were laws against anarchy, sedition, syndicalism.

KALB: It takes us perhaps I think to the 1964 ruling of the Supreme Court on *The New York Times v. Sullivan*, which is certainly called a landmark decision and you spoke earlier about the importance of libel at that time. And in this particular ruling, very specific regulations—that's the wrong word, but—concepts are written into this ruling and I'd like to just read what Justice Brennan has said because I think it deserves to be quoted as often as possible: "Public discussion is a political duty and it must be uninhibited, robust, and wide open and may well include vehement, caustic, and sometimes unpleasantly sharp attacks on government and public officials." And you were mentioning this in a sense a moment ago. And I'm wondering, Justice Scalia, if this kind of an issue were brought before the court today . . . At that time, in 1964, I believe the court's ruling was a 9–0, it was a unanimous vote. What would happen today?

SCALIA: I don't recall whether it was unanimous or not, I'm not sure if it was . . .

KALB: It was, it was 9–0. But I stand to be corrected!

SCALIA: Even so, it was wrong. [*Laughter*]

KALB: It was wrong?

SCALIA: The issue is not whether it's a good idea to let anybody—what *New York Times v. Sullivan* holds is that if you are a public figure—and it's been a matter of some doubt what it takes to become a public figure, but certainly any politician is a public figure—if you are a public figure, you cannot sue somebody for libel unless you can prove, effectively, that the person knew it was a lie. So long as he heard from somebody, you know . . . It makes it very difficult for a public figure to win a libel suit.

I think George Washington, I think Thomas Jefferson,

I think the framers would have been appalled at the notion that they could be libeled with impunity. And when the Supreme Court came out with that decision, it was revising the Constitution. Now, it may be a very good idea to set up a system that way, and New York State could have revised its libel laws by popular vote to say that if you libel a public figure it's okay unless it's malicious. But New York State didn't do that. It was nine lawyers who decided that's what the Constitution ought to mean, even though it had never meant that. And that's essentially the difference between Ruth and me concerning a living Constitution. She thinks that's all right, and I don't think it's all right.

GINSBURG: The situation didn't exist, in 1787 or 1791, that the Court confronted in *Times v. Sullivan*. The history in *Times v. Sullivan*, it was a sheriff who said he was libeled in an advertisement in the *New York Times*. It was in the midst of the civil rights era where libel laws could be used as a way of squelching the people who were asserting their freedom. So I think that *Times v. Sullivan* is a decision of major significance. Now I will say that the lawyer who argued that case for the *New York Times*, Herbert Wexler, a great constitutional law scholar, when its story is told, when he told Sulzberger, "We won, we won unanimously," Sulzberger's response was a little hesitant. He said, "It's great for the *New York Times*, but what about all those other papers that don't have our high standards." But I think that *Times v. Sullivan* is now well accepted and I quite disagree with my colleague. I suspect that if the Founding Fathers were around to see what life was like in America in the 1960s, they would have agreed with that.

KALB: So you would have voted for it?

SCALIA: Oh, god yes, she would have voted for it. [*Laughter*] Come on, come on, Mr. Kalb! [*Laughs*]

GINSBURG: I would mention it, but I won't say anything more about it because this a case we're going to hear next week I think. A state has passed a law that says, "Thou shall not make false statements in a political campaign against any candidate, any ballot initiative"—no false statements in elections. The question that the Court will face is: is that statute prohibiting false statements in political campaigns, is that constitutional?

KALB: What are we going to expect on that? [*Laughter*]

SCALIA: A decision by the end of June. [*Laughter*]

GINSBURG: It was another decision, and I don't remember where Justice Scalia was, but it was the Alvarez case. The man who lied about having the medal of honor—what was it called, something valor.

SCALIA: Stolen Valor Act.

GINSBURG: The Stolen Valor Act—

KALB: I want to point out that there's a new report out by an organization called Reporters Without Borders, very highly regarded, that the US has experienced what it called a "profound erosion of press freedom" in 2013, dropping 14 points to number 46 in global rankings.

Now, reporters are a little nervous these days and they like to feel that they have friends, and I want to know in your judgment whether reporters are right in considering the Supreme Court today as a friend of the concept of the freedom of the press.

SCALIA: You want me to say no to that? [*Laughter*] Of course everybody on the Court believes in the freedom of the press. Now there is some difference as to what that means. As to whether it means, for example, that a member of the press, no matter what the national emergency may be, need not disclose his or her source. That's a question that hasn't come up before us, and I think it's a very interesting, and not necessarily—not a question with a clear answer.

So, you know, you can believe in the freedom of the press and still have fun disagreeing, okay?

GINSBURG: I would like to know how it was determined that that was—that 46 was the US. I'm just thinking of the tradition in England which holds to this very day that the press can't report about trials, about ongoing trials.

SCALIA: And they can libel public figures in England.

KALB: Well since 1964 and the Sullivan-*New York Times* case, as you were pointing out before, it's extremely difficult now for anybody to libel a reporter on this issue. What I would like to get to here is something that is current and very important to an awful lot of people in this country and I suspect that the Court is going to face a number of major decisions in the area of government surveillance. The National Security Agency, the NSA, its newly disclosed activity and all of the problems of whistleblowing journalism and it's worth noting that the *Washington Post*, just this week, won its Pulitzer Prize for its reporting on Edward Snowden and the NSA. So I'd like to start by asking you, do you think the *Post* deserved the prize? Justice Ginsburg?

GINSBURG: That's a question that the journalists in this audience are much better equipped to answer than I am.

SCALIA: I don't read the *Post*, so I have no idea what they got the prize for. [*Laughter*]

GINSBURG: I do, including the announcement at the bottom of the first page that says what's coming up this week, and this evening was announced as an event.

SCALIA: Oh, very nice.

KALB: Yes it was, very proud of that. So tell me, I didn't get terribly far on that, do you believe that Snowden is a whistleblower or a traitor?

SCALIA: Oh, I don't, you know, that's not part of what I worry about, really. That's a policy question, not a legal question, and I stay out of that stuff.

GINSBURG: And it's also possible, is it not, that the question you raise could come before the Court.

KALB: That is possible.

GINSBURG: And we are not at liberty to preview . . .

KALB: No, I appreciate that. Let me ask the question from another angle. [*Laughter*]

SCALIA: If it's the same question, you're going to get the same answer!

KALB: That may be! That may be. [*Laughs*] But I'm going to try it anyway. If somebody were to say to you that, "What I am doing, you may disagree with"—I don't mean you personally, you all may disagree with—"but I am doing this because I feel a moral obligation to do this. I feel deep in my heart that my country is doing something wrong and I have an opportunity to change that and I want to change it."

SCALIA: So did the Germans who killed Jews, I mean, is that the criterion? Whether you honestly believe what you're doing is good? You have an obligation to form your conscience according to what is right. And that's the issue. The issue is whether it's right, not whether you believe in it. I'm sure Hitler was very sincere.

KALB: But the idea of it being right, you mean right according to the law as established?

SCALIA: Well in the context you put it, right according to—

KALB: Some moral judgment.

SCALIA: Right, to the Ten Commandments.

KALB: Right, okay.

GINSBURG: But we should note a point that was brought up before about hateful speech. There was a case some many years ago involving the town of Skokie, Illinois, where many Holocaust survivors lived, and the American Nazi party decided it would pick that town for a demonstration. The case never came to the US Supreme Court but other federal courts said the demonstration is going to be peaceful, there will be police protection, we don't anticipate any violence. This group wants to march, we hate what they say, but we believe in their freedom to say it.

SCALIA: But that doesn't mean it was good for them to say it, or right for them to say it. It sometimes annoys me when someone has made outrageous statements that are hateful. Somebody says—sometimes the press will say—"Well, he was just exercising his First Amendment rights." You know, as though, First Amendment rights are like muscles: the more you use them, the better. And it doesn't matter what purpose you're using them for. I mean, you could be using your First Amendment rights, and it can be abominable that you are using your First Amendment rights. I will defend your right to use it, but I will not defend the appropriateness of the manner in which you're using it now. That can be very wrong.

GINSBURG: Justice Scalia was praised by some, criticized by others for his decision in the flag-burning case. Now I imagine that you thought the act itself was reprehensible.

SCALIA: I would have sent that guy to jail if I was king. [*Laughter*]

KALB: But by your ruling, he had the right to burn the flag.

SCALIA: Yes, that's what the First Amendment means. You have the right to express your contempt for the government. It doesn't mean it was a good idea for him to do that in that manner, by burning a symbol that meant so much to so many other people. But he had the right to do it.

KALB: Justice Scalia, at a recent event in Brooklyn, you are quoted as saying that basically the Supreme Court should not be deciding matters of national security, and you're quoted as saying, "The Supreme Court does not know diddly about the nature and extent of the threat—"

SCALIA: "Diddly," did I say "diddly"? [*Laughter*]

KALB: That's what you're quoted as saying. "It's truly stupid," you went on, "that my court is going to be the last word on it." First of all, did you say that?

SCALIA: No, I think I probably did. I certainly believe it! [*Laughs*]

GINSBURG: I don't think we have a choice. The Court doesn't decide whether to pick this area and straighten it out today. There are petitions for review. And if there is a law that the government says was violated and the other side says, "No the government can't do this—can't engage in that kind of surveillance," and that case comes to us, we can't run away and say, "Well, we don't know much about that subject so we won't decide it."

SCALIA: You know what I was talking about, this related to the Fourth Amendment, not the Fifth Amendment. The Fourth Amendment which prohibits unreasonable searches and seizures. The first time my court had a case involving wiretapping, it held that the way the Fourth Amendment reads is "the people shall be secure in their persons, houses, papers, and effects—possessions—against unreasonable searches and seizures" and the court said, quite properly, "Hey, conversations are not persons, houses, papers and effects. Wiretapping may be a very bad thing, states may have laws against it, but it does not violate the federal Constitution. All right?

About twenty years later, during the Warren Court, we made an 180 degree turn, and we said there are penumbras and emanations and conversations are covered by this vague right of privacy that is contained in the Constitution. Now, that is the living Constitution: changing what the text says and what it originally meant. The consequence of that, I was pointing out in Brooklyn—I like Brooklyn—the consequence of that is that now the institution of the government that is going to decide this highly significant NSA question about what information you can get by wiretapping, the institution that will decide that is without a doubt the institution that is least qualified to decide that. It will be my court. It's a question of balancing the emergency against the intrusion. When the emergency is high enough, you can have a higher intrusion. It's why we all get searched when we board an airplane. That's a terrible intrusion—[*Ginsburg interjects*]—let me finish.

We know nothing about the degree of the risk. Nothing at all. The executive knows. The Congress knows. We don't know anything. And we're going to be the one to decide that question.

GINSBURG: So what do we do when the case comes to us? Before you answer that, I would like to remind everyone that in the wiretapping case, the argument that wiretapping was not an unreasonable search or seizure, there was a very strong opinion the other way by Justice Brandeis, and if I were on that court, I would have voted the way he did.

I would like to know how Justice Scalia distinguishes that kind of intrusion by the government from the decision you made in the heat emissions case. Now, the helicopter that was flying over roofs to test the level of heat, because if it was of a certain heat, then maybe marijuana plants were growing. The helicopter never touched the roof. And yet, you said, that was a violation of the Fourth Amendment.

SCALIA: Because the people were not being secure in their houses from unreasonable search. I mean that's a clear example of one of the facilities that is protected by the Fourth Amendment.

GINSBURG: So you can wiretap someone in their house?

SCALIA: Yeah, if you have to break into their house to wiretap. But if you listen in to conversations when they're in the phonebooth, oooh [*wiggles hands*], intruding about their generalized right of privacy. That was never covered by the Fourth Amendment.

GINSBURG: You don't have to worry about that anymore. There are no phone booths. [*Laughter*]

SCALIA: You're right about that, you're right about that.

KALB: Let me ask you this—

SCALIA: But anyway, we've gotten away from the Fifth Amendment haven't we.

KALB: No, I want to stick with this.

GINSBURG: First Amendment.

SCALIA: Oh, First Amendment, I'm sorry.

KALB: Stick with the Fourth Amendment just a sec. And I don't know terribly much about it and I can acknowledge that upfront, but my question is, could data that is considered terribly important either by the media or by the government stored in a computer or stored in a cloud up there somewhere, be considered effects—

SCALIA: Could be! That's very perceptive. I've thought about that—

KALB: And if—

SCALIA: I've thought about that—

KALB: Thank you, sir. Thank you—

SCALIA: You'd be a good lawyer—

KALB: But if you thought about that, doesn't it follow that the US government would not be able to justify its NSA surveillance program, and therefore conceivably could be in violation of the Constitution.

SCALIA: No, because it's not absolute. As Ruth said, there are very few freedoms that are absolute. I mean, your person is protected by the Fourth Amendment, but as I've pointed out, when you've boarded a plane, somebody can pass his hands all over your body. That's a terrible intrusion. But, given the danger that it's guarding against, it's not an unreasonable intrusion. And it can be the same thing with acquiring this data that is regarded as effects. And that's why I say it's foolish to have us make the decision, because I don't know how serious the danger is in this NSA stuff.

KALB: But don't you in the Supreme Court have the ability to pick up the phone and call somebody at the White House and I say, "I have a question about—"

GINSBURG: Absolutely not.

SCALIA: Absolutely not. [*Laughs*] We are at the mercy of whatever people happen to bring to us. If they don't bring it to us, we don't know it.

GINSBURG: And we can't make a decision based on something outside the record of the case. The parties and their lawyers have to know everything, have access to everything that we will factor into our decision. I don't know how many times I would have loved to call law professor so-and-so who is the biggest expert—

SCALIA: Call your husband in a tax case, for example.

GINSBURG: Right.

SCALIA: Marty was one of the best tax lawyers in the country.

GINSBURG: But we can't do that. Because the other sides, the parties aren't there. They don't have access to the same information. So we are hemmed in by the record of the case and the court cannot resort to information that the parties do not have.

KALB: Justice Ginsburg, I want to ask you the same question that I asked Justice Scalia about the data, the storage in computers, and linking that to the word "effects," and if that is justifiably linked to the word "effects," doesn't it follow logically that the case could be made that the government is in violation of the Constitution by this government surveillance program?

GINSBURG: An argument could be made, certainly, but it's not an argument that either of us can answer. Well I think, Justice Scalia suggested we can't answer at all. I don't think that's so. We have to answer it and we will. But we don't get questions in the form you pose them, Marvin. We get a concrete case, and not an abstract question. The effects are up there, what can the government do.

SCALIA: I would answer that one Ruth. That is "persons, houses, papers and effects." It's not, it's not conversations.

GINSBURG: But you couldn't answer it in the abstract.

SCALIA: Oh, certainly not. Certainly not.

KALB: Can we expect the Supreme Court to rule on the NSA issue?

GINSBURG: It depends if there is a case that will begin not in the Supreme Court but in the federal district court.

KALB: Ok, ok.

GINSBURG: And then go to a court of appeals. We do have the luxury of not having to decide things until they've been decided by other good minds. By judges in the federal trial courts and the courts of appeals.

SCALIA: And it's not our responsibility to shape up the executive and make sure they're doing what they're supposed to, or shaping up the Congress. That's not our job. Our job is to prevent people from being harmed. If nobody is being harmed, we don't get into the matter. And even if somebody is harmed, unless he comes to us, we don't have any self-starting powers. We're at the mercy of whoever wants to bring a case or whoever doesn't want to bring a case. Ruth and I visited India one time, a long time ago, and the Indian supreme court, India has a bill of rights which says that the Apex Court, their supreme court, will assure the preservation of the liberties set forth in the bill of rights, and that court interpreted that to mean that if they're sitting around on a Sunday, reading the *Bombay Times*, and they see that the police commissioner—

GINSBURG: Mumbai.

SCALIA: No, I—look, I—[*Laughter*]—I don't say "Par-eeh" and I don't say "Veeen" and I will not say "Mumbai." It's Bombay, we have an English word for it. Anyway, they're sitting around reading the *Bombay Times*, and they see that the police commissioner in Punjab is holding people without charge which violates the constitution. That court will, on its own, summon the police commissioner to give an account of himself. Our court can't do that, we can't do that. It's only when people bring problems to us.

KALB: You can't do that because that's the way it's always been done? Or there's a rule that says you can't do it?

GINSBURG: We can't because the Constitution limits us to actual cases and controversies. There are many courts in the world that do operate by answering abstract, general questions. Constitutional courts have been set up, there's a constitutional council in France that will preview a law. If a certain number of deputies question the consistency of the bill with the constitution, the council will look at the bill, no actual case before them, just look at the words of the bill, decide whether it's compatible with the constitution. And if the council holds it isn't compatible with the constitution, then the bill never gets enacted. But that kind of judicial preview is foreign to us.

KALB: Let's talk for a minute or so about televising hearings of the Supreme Court.

SCALIA: [*wiggles hands*] Ooooh.

GINSBURG: [*Laughs*]

KALB: Other courts do permit television. Why not the Supreme Court? Justice Scalia?

SCALIA: You know, when I first came on the Court, I was in favor of it. I have long since changed my view on that. Those who want to do it say they want to educate the American people. Now if I really thought it would educate the American people, I would be in favor of it. And indeed if the American people watched our proceedings from gavel to gavel, they would be educated. They would come to realize that although we do now and then do these sexy cases, "Should there be a right to abortion?" "Should there be a right to suicide?" "Should there be a right to this or that?"

Most of the time, we are not contemplating our navel. We are not engaging in this broad philosophical, ethical search. Most of the time, we are doing real law. We are doing the internal revenue code, the bankruptcy code, ERISA, really dull stuff. [*Laughter*] And nobody would ever again come up to me and say, "Justice Scalia, why do you have to be a lawyer to be on the Supreme Court." Because they think we're looking up at the sky and saying, "Should this right or that right exist." Well they can guess that as well as I can. Now, the problem is for every person who watches us from gavel to gavel, there will be 10,000 who watch a fifteen- or thirty-second take-out on the nightly news and I guarantee you that will not be characteristic of what we do. It will be man-bites-dog.

So why should I participate in the miseducation of the American people?

KALB: [*to Ginsburg*] What about your feelings?

GINSBURG: There's another factor. If you are televising a trial, everything that's unfolding is before the camera. If you're dealing with an appellate argument—well, if you would come to our chambers at the moment, because we're starting a sitting on Monday, you will see carts with briefs and briefs and briefs. The oral argument in court is fleeting. It is only thirty minutes a side. I don't know how many hours we have spent preparing, reading what had gone on the case before it got to the Supreme Court, reading the briefs that the parties filed, and the many friends of court who want to be heard on questions of importance to them.

So the notion that an appellate argument is a contest between lawyers and the better one will win is really a false picture of what the appellate process is.

KALB: So you would be, as Justice Scalia, opposed to the televising.

GINSBURG: I think it's probably inevitable, because there's going to be so much pressure for it and because other courts do it. But I would be very much concerned with mis-portraying what an appeal is. The written part is ever so much more important than the hour total in court.

KALB: In the couple minutes we have left, I want to just ask a question. You've both been great buddies for a while now, but when did you meet and what were the circumstances.

GINSBURG: I bet he doesn't know. [*Laughter*]

SCALIA: Go ahead, Ruth. Go on.

KALB: When did you meet?

GINSBURG: We were buddies on the DC Circuit.

KALB: And that is when you met, at that time?

GINSBURG: I met Nino for the first time when he was giving a speech to some unit of the ABA. It must have been the administrative law section, probably. And it was on a case that had recently been decided by the DC circuit. It was before either of us got there. And it was about—

SCALIA: We were both academics, I'm sorry.

GINSBURG: Yea, it was about the Vermont Yankee case. And you were, in vain, against it.

SCALIA: Terrible decision.

GINSBURG: And I was listening to him and disagreeing with a good part of what he said. But thought he said it in an absolutely captivating way. [*Laughter*]

SCALIA: [*Laughs*]

KALB: I think we should leave it at that. Great point. I mean, as you know, composer Derrick Wang, who is with us tonight, has produced this opera called "Scalia/Ginsburg" and in it, to beautiful music, you're both locked in a room, I understand, unable to get out unless you agree on a compromise consistent with the Constitution. And at one point Scalia roars in despair, "Oh, Ruth, can you read? You're aware of the text yet so proudly you are unable to derive its true meaning. The Constitution says absolutely nothing about this." To which Ginsburg replies, "How many times must I tell you, dear Mr. Justice Scalia, you are searching in vain for a bright-line solution, but the beautiful thing about our Constitution, is that like our society, it can evolve." So we've got only about a minute or so left: are you two ever going to agree on big issues? And still maintain the friendship?

SCALIA: We agree on a whole lot of stuff. Ruth is really bad only on the knee-jerk stuff. [*Laughter*] She's a really good textualist, and those things where the text is what she's guided by, she's terrific. Obviously very smart and most cases, I think, we're together. I think we're together on a lot of criminal defense cases, upholding the rights of the criminal defendant. Ruth and I are quite frequently in dissent from the Court's decision.

So no, we agree on a whole lot. You have it wrong.

KALB: I keep seeing these 5–4 decisions—

GINSBURG: There are major—

KALB: —where you're on one side and she's on the other—

GINSBURG: Well that's because the press focuses on, what, the 20 to 25 percent of the heady cases, the constitutional cases. Most of what we're doing is—

SCALIA: Real law.

GINSBURG: —trying to interpret dense statutes that Congress passed that are very difficult to parse and on those cases there isn't the usual lineup that the press expects to see in the most-watched cases. So we agree on many procedure cases, not always. You got one wrong last year. [*Scalia and Ginsburg laugh*]

And also I have to say something else. We both care about the way opinions are crafted. It's not easy to write an opinion. And I think you care very much about how it's said. And so do I. Of course, the way we say it is quite different.

SCALIA: And one reason we became such good friends on the DC circuit was that we were both former academics. I guess Harry Edwards was another academic on the court. But in academia, at law school, when you wrote a law review article, you would circulate it to your colleagues, and they would make comments—helpful comments. Not just, "This is wrong." But, you know, "There's an additional point you could make." Well, Ruth and I did that with one another's opinions. We wouldn't do it to anyone else's, but she would suggest some additional stuff that I could put in and I would for her as well.

KALB: I would like us to go on, but our time's up. I'm sorry about that. I want to thank our wonderful, attentive audience. I want to thank the many who watched and listened all over the nation and the world. But most importantly, I want to thank our remarkable guests, two sitting justices of the Supreme Court of the United States, Antonin Scalia and Ruth Bader Ginsburg. Thank you both, so much.

CINEMA CAFE WITH RUTH BADER GINSBURG & NINA TOTENBERG

INTERVIEW BY NINA TOTENBERG
SUNDANCE FILM FESTIVAL, PARK CITY, UTAH
JANUARY 21, 2018

ROBERT REDFORD: Hi everyone. I'm here because I have the pleasure and the honor of introducing our guest today: Ruth Bader Ginsburg, Justice. [*Applause*] It's an honor for me especially because I have such a long history of admiration for her for so long. And so to be able to be with her today and welcome her to our festival, I think she's going to enhance the quality of our festival just by being here, so I'm happy to introduce her. And let me just say that there are many reasons to celebrate and honor her. I would be here for a long, long time if I listed all the attributes that she had, but let me just state a couple. The fact that she was born in poverty, near poverty, and rose up through the ranks from the lower rung on the ladder, so to speak, to rise up to become a woman in a world of law dominated by men, and to continue to rise so she became a Supreme Court justice. And to watch her, and what her qualities are—the fight for justice and equality are the two main things I can think of. But I can't think of any greater honor than to be able to introduce a person I so admire—Supreme Court Justice Ruth Bader Ginsburg.

JOHN NEIN: I'm here to welcome you to Cinema Café. My name is John Nein, I'm a senior programmer of the festival. I'm very grateful for our guests joining us today. I think this is obviously a highlight of the festival for all of us, and I say that because, over the ten days of this festival a lot of the focus is on the films and the screening of new independent work. But I think from our point of view also those films incite conversation, and we've always seen the festival as a place that is a place of dialogue, it's a place of ideas, it's a place for us to process the work that we're seeing and sort of reconcile what that means for our lives in our society, so we're really, really happy to be hosting this conversation. And I want to thank our moderator for the conversation, Nina Totenberg. [*Applause*] Nina Totenberg, who many of us know from her voice several times a week on NPR. And those select few carry our things around in the "Nina Totenbag." So thank you so much Nina, and thank you Justice Ginsburg. Thank you all for coming.

NINA TOTENBERG: Well I, for one, am delighted to be here with Justice Ginsburg. She is perhaps the most recognizable justice on the Supreme Court, though she underweighs them all, even the women, probably by about forty pounds. So even before she became the second woman to serve on the nation's highest court, Ruth Ginsburg quite simply changed the way the world is for American women.

For more than a decade until her first judicial appointment in 1980, she led the fight in the courts for gender equality. When she began her legal crusade, women were treated *by law* differently from men. Thousands of state and federal laws treated women differently from men. They restricted what women could do, barring them from jobs, rights, even from jury duty. By the time she first put on judicial robes, however, she had worked a revolution. So, let's start with what's going on in the world of women today. You were the architect of the legal fight for women's rights. Today the issues are both the same and different. Different is that front and center is the question of sexual harassment: how to treat various kinds of behavior; what should be a fireable offense, a lesser offense; can offenders redeem themselves; whether peers in the workplace can date; and on, and on, and on. But what I want to know first is whether when you were a younger woman, not a judge or a Supreme Court justice, were you ever subject to inappropriate behavior, and how did you handle it?

JUSTICE RUTH BADER GINSBURG: The answer is yes. Every woman of my vintage knows what sexual harassment is, although we didn't have a name for it. But if I can just preface my remarks about sexual harassment with my first introduction to Nina Totenberg. And I think it must have been 1971, I was teaching at Rutgers Law School. Nina called me and said, "I'd like to ask you a question. What does this equal protection got to do with women? I thought the Equal Protection Clause of the Fourteenth Amendment is about race. How does it apply to women?" And that was our first conversation, and we have been close friends ever since. [*Applause*]

The attitude to sexual harassment was simply, "Get past it, boys will be boys." Well I'll give you just one example. I'm taking a chemistry course at Cornell and my instructor said—because I was uncertain of my ability in that field—he said "I'll give you a practice exam." So he gave me a practice exam. The next day, on the test, the test is the practice exam and I knew exactly what he wanted in return. And that's just one of many examples.

This was not considered anything you could do

something about, that the law could help you do something about until a book was written a then-young woman named Kitty MacKinnon, Catherine MacKinnon, and it was called *Sexual Harassment in the Workplace*, and I was asked to read it by a publisher and give my opinion on whether it was worth publishing. It was a revelation. The first part described incidents like the one I just mentioned, and the next was how this anti-discrimination law, Title VII—which prohibits discrimination on the basis of race, national origin, religion, and sex—how that could be used as a tool to stop sexual harassment. It was eye-opening and it was the beginning of a field that didn't exist until then.

TOTENBERG: So, just to close the loop here, for a minute, what did you do about the professor? Did you just stay clear of him? What did you do?

GINSBURG: I went to his office and I said, "How dare you! How dare you do this!" [*Applause*] And that was the end of that.

TOTENBERG: [*Laughs*] I assume you did quite well on that exam!

GINSBURG: And when I deliberately made two mistakes! [*Laughter*]

TOTENBERG: What are your thoughts about what women should be doing now? I deliberately left in a lot of the questions, because it is more complicated than people may think at first blush, and I wonder what you think of the Me Too movement and if you've given any thought to the strategy for women as a group.

GINSBURG: Well, I think it's about time, and for so long women were silent, thinking there was nothing you could do about it. But now the law is on the side of women, or men, who encounter harassment and that's a good thing.

TOTENBERG: In the film industry, it turns out that a lot of women aren't being paid as well as men, or at least that their agents don't push for them to be paid as well as men. There have been a couple times in your career, first at Rutgers Law School and then at Columbia, when you found out that you and other women and, in a third case, female janitors were not being treated the same as men. In two cases you sued them and in the third case you threatened to—weren't you worried that they would fire you?

GINSBURG: Being paid the same as men . . . When I joined the faculty of Rutgers Law School, Rutgers is a state university, and the dean, who was a very kindly man, said, "Ruth, you're going to have to take a cut in salary." And I said, "I understand that. State universities don't pay so well," but when he told me how much of a cut I was astonished. So I asked, "Well, how much do you pay so-and-so?"—a man, who was out of law school about the same amount of time I was—and the dean replied, "Ruth, he has a wife and two children to support. You have a husband with a good-paying job in New York!" That was the very year the Equal Pay Act had passed—that was the answer that I got.

What the women at Rutgers did was, they didn't make a big fuss. They got together and they filed an Equal Pay Act complaint, not even Title VII, just straight Equal Pay. So that suit was filed in 1964. The university settled. The lowest increase was $6,000, which in those days was a lot more than it is today. When I got to Columbia, one problem was with the faculty, because the university didn't give out salary figures. I was the law school's representative to the University Senate and the first thing we wanted to get was those figures, and then once we did, our case was won.

The maids-janitor situation is, I get to Columbia, this is—what year was it—1972, and a feminist I knew well came to see me to tell me that Columbia had just issued twenty-five layoff notices to twenty-five women in the maintenance department, no layoffs for any men. And then she said to me, "What are you going to do about it?" So I went to the university vice president for business and told him that the university was violating Title VII, and he said, "Professor Ginsburg, Columbia has excellent Wall Street lawyers representing them, and would you like a cup of tea?"

Well, that was on a Monday, and there was an application to stop Columbia immediately, to get a temporary injunction. There was a meeting at Columbia with feminists—at that meeting Bella Abzug was there, Gloria Steinem was there, Susan Sontag was there. I think that so impressed the Equal Employment Opportunity Commission that they sent their chief counsel to argue in favor of the temporary injunction.

We get to court on Monday morning. The union— one of Columbia's excuses was—the union wanted to have separate seniority lines so that we had janitors and maids, and no janitor would be let go until all the maids were gone. So Columbia said, "The union insisted on that in our contract." The union representative got up in court and said, "We can't abide by a contract that violates Title VII." So the union came over on the side of the maids and Columbia was there, all alone.

And of course there was a temporary injunction, but the most heartening thing about it was the women who were categorized as maids. These are women who really didn't care that they were paid less, they expected that, but they wanted jobs. They didn't want to be on welfare. In the course of that litigation those women grew in self-esteem, and two of them ended up being shop stewards, and that was the most heartening part of the maids-janitor controversy.

When Columbia lost and the preliminary injunction was issued, Columbia decided, well they really didn't have to lay off anyone. They could take care of the excess numbers by attrition, by not hiring a replacement for someone who left. So when they were faced with the necessity of having to drop about ten men before they reached the first woman, they found a way to avoid laying off anyone.

TOTENBERG: You know, there's no doubt in all of these situations who is the backbone of the opposition, the legal backbone—it's you, so how come they didn't fire you?

GINSBURG: My troops at the law school were hugely supportive, and I think the university knew I was untouchable for that reason. Whatever I did, and the faculty was behind me, even if they disagreed. And the one time we had a serious disagreement was in the pension case. So in those days when women retired they got less than men per month—

TOTENBERG: —because they live longer.

GINSBURG: Right, so they were actuarially equal. So the whole idea of Title VII is you don't lump-categorize people. And it's true that on average women live longer than men. But there are some women who die young, and some men who live past 100.

TOTENBERG: So how did they treat—were they mad at you over that?

GINSBURG: Yes, they were concerned that they would get less per month than they would otherwise when they retired.

TOTENBERG: So, do you ever worry with the Me Too movement about a backlash against women?

GINSBURG: Let's see where it goes. So far, it's been great. Yes and there was a book—what was her name, the one who wrote the book called *Backlash*—

AUDIENCE: Susan Faludi.

GINSBURG: —Faludi, yes. But when I see women appearing every place in numbers, I'm less worried about backlash than I might have been twenty years ago.

TOTENBERG: So we're here at Sundance, a center of one form of the arts, so let me ask you: do you remember the first movie that you really loved, and if there's some movie in the last few years that you really loved?

GINSBURG: Well, the first movie, that's an easy question. It was *Gone with the Wind*. I don't know whether I would have loved it if I saw it today, but I saw it at least five times.

TOTENBERG: What about now?

GINSBURG: It's hard to pick out one film. Of course—well, I'll just say the two most recent films I saw. I don't get a chance to go to the movies very often, but one was *Three Billboards [Outside Ebbing, Missouri]*, a fantastic film. And the other was *Call Me By Your Name*, which is a beautiful, beautiful film. I have to find out where in Italy it took place!

TOTENBERG: Some people here may not know about your devotion to other art forms like the opera. You once told me if you could be anything in the world you would have been an operatic diva. So why weren't you?

GINSBURG: Because I'm a monotone! [*Laughs*] But in my dreams, that's a recurring dream. I'm onstage at the Metropolitan Opera, and I'm about to sing *Tosca*, and then I remember that I am a monotone!

TOTENBERG: What is it about opera and music in general that has so captivated you, that on any given night in Washington, at least once or twice a week I would guess, you're at the opera, or the symphony, or some other musical performance?

GINSBURG: Most recently, Wednesday night of this week, I was at the dress rehearsal of a new opera, called *Proving Up*.

I was turned on to opera when I was eleven years old. I was a grade-school kid in Brooklyn, and my aunt took me to a children's performance of a most unlikely choice for a first opera. It was *La Gioconda*. These were operas condensed to one hour. There were costumes, there was bare staging, and there was a narrator who was also the conductor of an all-childrens' orchestra. That man's name was Dean Dixon. The year was 1944.

Dean Dixon left the United States at the end of the forties and commented that, for all the time he'd been conducting, no one had ever called him maestro. Why? Because he was African American. So he went off to Europe and he was the darling of every major orchestra there, he married well, and some twenty years later, he came back to the United States, at the end of the sixties, just to visit. And every major symphony orchestra in the country wanted him to be a guest conductor. And that illustrates for me, the enormous change in our country from the middle forties to the late sixties.

Anyway, I got hooked on opera at age eleven, I began to attend the rehearsals at the City Center in New York.

TOTENBERG: What does it do for you? What does music do for you?

GINSBURG: What does it do? What does beautiful music do?

It takes me out of my immediate concerns, out of worrying about how I'm going to write this opinion so that it will be understood by the audience. It is enchanting. I tend to listen to the music both in chambers, either a CD or the one classical station we have in DC. Sometimes I have to turn it off because I have to think really, really hard, and can't have any distractions.

TOTENBERG: You know, if you walk into the justice's chambers, I think any of you in this room would be quite surprised. Supreme Court justices are allowed to have artwork from the National Gallery, anything that they want, that's not on the walls of the National Gallery. So they can say, "I'd like this or that" and it's loaned to them until the National Gallery might need it for an exhibition or something like that. And most of the artwork is fairly traditional artwork. You walk into her chambers and it's all extremely modern artwork. What is it you love about modern art?

GINSBURG: Well first, my colleagues' taste runs in two directions. One is portraits—portraits of long-dead men. [*Laughter*] And the other is outdoor scenes. It's not just the National Gallery—I have two paintings from the National Gallery. I have five from the Museum of American Art. And I was allowed to go downstairs at the Gallery, to see the huge collection of Mark Rothkos they have. You would not recognize my paintings as Mark Rothko's because he changed his style so very much. The five that I have from the Museum of American Art come from something called the Frost Collection. It's a collection of United State painters in the WPA period roughly from 1933 to 1945. And so I have five of those. And I have one from the Hirshhorn.

TOTENBERG: The film that's being premiered here today about you, I thought I'd ask you about a little bit. Now, neither of us has seen it. And you don't want to talk about it because you haven't seen it. So I thought I'd ask you about the process of being followed around by cameras for a while. You're used to public appearances and even public interviews, but how is that? And did you dress any differently?

GINSBURG: Did I dress for the camera? No. [*Laughs*] I think Betsy and Julie wanted me to be just as I am. Well, you'll see in the film. As Nina told you, neither of us has seen it yet, but I have great expectations.

TOTENBERG: I know the film crew played for you a video of your own self being portrayed on *Saturday Night Live*, and your children told them that you had not ever seen it. So what did you think of your portrayal on *Saturday Night Live*?

GINSBURG: I like the actress who portrayed me.

TOTENBERG: I think it's Kate McKinnon.

GINSBURG: Yea, and I would like to say [*in a nasal voice*] "Ginz-burg" sometimes to my colleagues.

TOTENBERG: You know this brings something up. At age 84, you're going strong—as you can see everybody, she hasn't dropped a stitch—and every liberal in America is prepared to throw their bodies in front of you to protect you. [*Applause*] You are a rock star, there are songs about you, T-shirts, mugs, you're now known simply as the Notorious RBG. This must be fun for you, but how do you suppose your colleagues feel?

GINSBURG: My colleagues are judiciously silent about the Notorious RBG.

TOTENBERG: So let me go back to when you weren't a rock star and you were at Cornell in undergraduate school and you met the man who would be your husband, Marty Ginsburg. Now, back then, men far, far outnumbered women at Cornell. So what was it about Marty that struck your fancy?

GINSBURG: First, men outnumbering women: there were four men to every woman at Cornell in those days. So it was the ideal school for the parents of daughters because if you couldn't get your man at Cornell, you were hopeless. [*Laughter*]

Well the remarkable thing about Marty, to whom I was married for 56 years, is he cared that I had a brain. No guy up until then was the least interested in how I thought. So Marty was a revelation to me. And throughout my life, I certainly wouldn't be here today were it not for Marty because he made me feel that I was better than I thought I was.

When I went to law school, I was concerned in those first few weeks whether I would make it. Marty was telling—he was a year ahead of me—he was telling all of his buddies, "My wife will be on the law review." Well that's just how he was.

He had a great sense of humor and, another very important strength, he was a wonderful cook. And he said he owed
his skill in the kitchen to two women: at first his mother and
then his wife. I thought he gave his mother a bum rap but he
was certainly right about me. And now there is, at the Supreme Court gift shop, a book called *Supreme Chef.* That supreme chef is Marty Ginsburg. The spouses of my colleagues,
when Marty died, thought that the best tribute they could
have to him would be a collection of his recipes.

TOTENBERG: So Marty Ginsburg was a great gourmet chef.
He wasn't just a great chef. I mean he really was stupendous.
At the same time that he was one of the country's leading tax
experts and one of the funniest men alive.

But you went to Harvard Law School together. He was a
year ahead of you. And you were just one of nine women in a
class of over 500. You were on law review. You had a fourteen-
month-old daughter. And then Marty was diagnosed with
testicular cancer. The doctors threw the book at him, what
they had at the time, which was massive radiation. And he
was pretty sick—

GINSBURG: Massive surgery first.

TOTENBERG: Massive surgery and radiation, and he was
pretty sick. How did you manage to get through that time?
What was the routine that you established for yourself?

GINSBURG: How I got through that time was mainly his
classmates and mine. Harvard Law School was supposed to

be fiercely competitive. Our experience was quite different. My classmates, his classmates rallied around us and helped us get through that very difficult time.

Marty's routine with radiation—it was massive radiation, there was no such thing as chemotherapy then. So he'd get the radiation, come home, be terribly sick, fall asleep, and get up about midnight. I had between midnight and two when he went back to sleep. Whatever he was going to ingest that day, he was going to eat between those hours. And my routine was, I went to my classes. I had note-takers in all of his classes. I went to Mass General when he was at the hospital. And I came home, fed my daughter, she went to sleep, and I studied what I could for that time. Marty would get up. He would have some not very spectacular hamburger that I made, and then I would go back to the books again. So I learned to get by on very little sleep. Two hours a night was about it. That's what our routine was like, and I must say that Marty attended two weeks of classes that semester. He got the highest grades he ever got. He was very close to the top of his class. And that was because he had the best tutors in the world—his classmates—who took notes and then came to the hospital and then later home to give him tutorials.

TOTENBERG: So when he graduated, he got a good job in New York. You moved to New York, you went to Columbia for your last year. You graduated tied for first in your class there. And you had lots of recommendations for clerkships but most judges wouldn't even interview you. Indeed, even Supreme Court justices wouldn't interview you. So, how did you finally get a clerkship.

GINSBURG: I had a teacher at Columbia Law School, Gerald Gunther, who later moved to Stanford. He was in charge of getting clerkships for Columbia law students and he was determined to get a clerkship for me. He concentrated on one judge in the southern district of New York, a trial court judge, who was a graduate of Columbia College and Columbia Law School and took all of his clerks from Columbia.

When Gerry proposed me, the judge was hesitant. He said he had a woman law clerk and he said she was fine. He had one. But I had a then-four-year-old child, and so he was concerned that I couldn't do the job. I couldn't be there when he needed me because I would be taking care of my child if she were sick. So the professor made an offer to the judge. He said, "If you give her a chance, I have arranged for a young man in her class who is going to a Wall Street firm. If she doesn't work out, he'll jump in and take over." That was the carrot. And then there was a stick. And the stick was, "if you don't give her a chance, I will never recommend another Columbia student to you." Now this is a story I never knew about. I thought the judge had hired me because he had two daughters and he was thinking how he would like the world to be for them. It wasn't until Gerry wrote a comment in the *Hawai'i Law Journal* that I knew how I got that first job.

That was the challenge for women of my era. Getting your foot in the door. Getting that first job. Once you got that job, you did it at least as well, in many cases better, than the men. But it was the first job that was powerfully hard to get.

TOTENBERG: So tell the story about how you used to ride in the car with your judge and another judge, the very famous Learned Hand who had refused to hire you, was in the car also.

GINSBURG: Learned Hand was one of the greatest federal judges of all time. He was a brilliant man. My judge lived around the corner from Judge Hand and would drive him when Hand became an octogenarian. Judge Palmieri, my judge, would drive him to the courthouse and then back at the end of the day. And when I finished my work on time, I sat in the back of the car as they drove uptown. And I would hear this great man say whatever came into his head. Sing saucy songs. Salty songs. [*Laughs*] And I said to him, "You won't hire me as a clerk, but yet you say in this car—you don't inhibit your speech at all. You have said words that my mother never taught me." And he said, "Young lady, I am not looking at you." Men of that age were told, do inhibit your speech when you're talking to women.

TOTENBERG: But you were in the back seat. So he wasn't looking at you. So you weren't there. [*Laughs*] So I will leave to the movie the story of your professional career because we're getting low on time, but eventually you founded the ACLU Women's Project at the same time you were teaching at Columbia and litigating cases all over the country, and arguing cases in the Supreme Court. You had two children and there's a story I often get you to tell young women who are struggling with so-called life balance issues. It's a story about your son, James, in school.

GINSBURG: My son, James, who is now a really fine human, and makes the best classical CDs in the world. Chicago Classical Recording Foundation. This child was what his teachers called, hyperactive and I called lively. So I would get called by the head of the school or the school psychologist or the room teacher to come down immediately to hear about my son's latest escapade. Well one day, I think I'd been up all night writing a brief. I was at my office at Columbia Law School. I got the call and I responded, "This child has two parents. Please alternate calls. And it's his father's turn." So my husband, Marty, went down to the school, was confronted by three stone faces: the principal, the room teacher, the psychologist. And he was told, "Your son stole the elevator." It was one of those [manually operated] elevators. The elevator operator had gone out for a smoke, and one of my son's classmates dared him to take the kindergarteners up to the top floor in the elevator.

So Marty's response when he was told of this grave infraction on my son's part, Marty's response was, "He stole the elevator. How far could he take it?" Well I don't know if it was Marty's sense of humor, I suspect it was that the school was reluctant to take a man away from his work—it wouldn't hesitate to call a mother away from hers—anyway, there was no quick change in my son's behavior, but the calls came barely once a semester. And the reason was they had to think long and hard before asking a man to take time out of his workday to come to the school. [*Applause*]

TOTENBERG: You know, one of your great friends on the court was Justice Scalia, with whom you disagreed a great deal. But you were also very close friends and people often find it hard to understand that. How it was that this symbol of so-called originalism or textualism or conservatism on the Supreme Court and you were such close friends. So what was it about him that made you such close friends? I mean, he said of you, "What's not to like?" But what was it that you loved about him? And you did love him in many ways.

GINSBURG: Number one, his sense of humor. But the first time I heard, it was then professor, Scalia speak, it was at some lawyer's convention in Washington DC. I disagreed with a good deal of what he said, but I was captivated by the way, the way he said it. When we were buddies on the US court of appeals on the District of Columbia circuit—there were only three judges—and Nino would lean over and say something that absolutely cracked me up. And I had all I could do to avoid bursting out with laughter. So often I pinched myself very hard. So he has a great sense of humor. We both really care about families. And we share a love of beautiful music, especially opera.

TOTENBERG: You describe one of your opinions that you'll hear more about in the film, the VMI case, and your interaction with him—because he dissented, I think he was the sole dissenter. Describe that.

GINSBURG: He was the sole dissenter, I should say because Justice Thomas's son at the time was attending VMI, so he didn't sit on the case. So Nino ended up being the sole dissenter. I had circulated my opinion. I think we have somebody here who knows a little about it who can confirm. I think it was early in April when we circulated the opinion? And we were waiting on the dissent. It was time for me to go to my circuit judicial conference at Lake George, and Justice Scalia comes into my chambers, throws down a sheaf of paper on my desk and says, "Ruth, this is the penultimate draft of my VMI dissent. I'm not quite ready to circulate, but I want to give you as much time as I can to answer it."

So I took this draft on the plane with me to Albany. The conference was in Lake George. He absolutely ruined my weekend. But I was glad to have the extra days to answer him. I think we must have gone through about fifteen, sixteen drafts. It was a ping-pong game. Scalia would say such things as—I refer to the University of Virginia that finally admitted women in 1970–71, and I referred to the school as the University of Virginia at Charlottesville—he came back with, "There is no University of Virginia at Charlottesville. There is just the University of Virginia." And then explained in not quite these words that a kid from Brooklyn would understandably make such a mistake because she knew about the City University at New York, at Buffalo. Anyway, in the end, in that debate, I certainly proved right didn't I? VMI is thriving today.

TOTENBERG: It is. I urge you all to see the movie here, and if you can't get in to see the movie here, to see it when it's in theaters or on CNN. And I have known Ruth Bader Ginsburg for well over forty years. And the person you see here is very dignified and, as you can tell, she also has a great sense of humor. But what you may not know about her is she's a great human being. When my late husband died, and I started to date the doctor I am now married to, I remember walking down the hall one day with Justice Ginsburg at something she'd scooped me up to take me to, and I said "Ruth, I've started to date a doctor in Boston." And in my mind's eye, I remember her head spinning around and what she said was, "Details. I want all the details." So thank you Justice Ginsburg.

RUTH BADER GINSBURG IN HER OWN WORDS

INTERVIEW BY JANE EISNER
THE FORWARD
ADAS ISRAEL SYNAGOGUE, WASHINGTON, D.C.
FEBRUARY 1, 2018

JANE EISNER: Thank you all. Thank you to everyone coming here to Adas Israel.

It is such a thrill and a pleasure for me and on behalf of all of my colleagues to participate in such an important event. In the last few weeks, we've asked *Forward* readers to send us their questions for Justice Ginsburg. And the response has been overwhelming. We heard from readers all across the country and from overseas as well. Tonight I will quote from some of these questions in our conversation because they are brilliant and funny and they're a powerful reflection of how interested Americans truly are in the United States Supreme Court, and especially in this United States Supreme Court justice.

I do want to say at the outset that Justice Ginsburg has asked that we not discuss issues that are before the court or may be before the court.

And of course we're respecting that. Happily there are so many other topics to talk about. Justice Ginsburg, many readers of ours are interested in your Jewish life and identity and how it shaped your judicial career and your outlook. And as we sit in this beautiful sanctuary this seems like a very good place to start. You grew up in Brooklyn from a family . . . OK, let's hear it for Brooklyn. A family that was not devout, but very identified. You have described your mother, your beloved mother, lighting candles on Friday nights.

And I've heard how you've enjoyed celebrating Passover with your family. You've remarked that the four questions was the best part of the Seder. I'm wondering why.

JUSTICE RUTH BADER GINSBURG: A child—the youngest child—is asking about this evening, this celebration: "Why is Passover night different from all other nights?" It's a child asking a question and the rest of the Seder is devoted to answering it. The child's question.

I think it's just one of many illustrations of how Jews honor learning and want children to be well-educated.

EISNER: A couple of years ago with Rabbi Holtzblatt you wrote about the heroic and visionary women in the Passover story, and I'm just wondering, did you notice all that when you were a girl? Or is that the kind of thing that emerged later in life for you, this recognition of the role of women in this story?

GINSBURG: Well, Lauren* was the prime mover in this venture. I think growing up I might have known about Miriam and Moses' mother, but I didn't know about the midwives Shifra and Puah, and I knew about the Pharaoh's daughter. But the Passover Seder, the Haggadah, there were no women.

EISNER: That's true. And so you've worked to make a difference in that regard. And I understand that was something

---

* Lauren Holtzblatt, the rabbi of Adas Israel.

that you were aware of as a girl as well. Your limitations. The boys were having bar mitzvahs and girls could not. And your mother had a very strict Orthodox upbringing. And I'm just wondering how that experience of being a girl at a time when girls and women had very little or no role in religious life . . . how did that affect you? Did it inspire you or was it something that you wanted to change?

GINSBURG: Of course. Of course I wanted to change it, I wanted to have a big party for a bat mitzvah and get all those presents!

I grew up with a cousin. We lived in the same household. Two sisters married, two brothers who were three months apart. We were like twins and he was bar mitzvah'd. And had this great party. And all the gifts. I was very jealous.

EISNER: I've read that you traced the Jewish presence on the Supreme Court beginning not with Justice Louis Brandeis, the first justice, but actually with Judah Benjamin, who was the first Jew to be offered a seat in the United States Supreme Court—but who declined. And, in fact, he became a leader of the Confederacy. I'm wondering, why do you start there in thinking about the Jewish presence on the court?

GINSBURG: I don't think of Benjamin as present on the court. Jews come in all sizes and shapes and some are very good and some are not so good. Benjamin was a very interesting character—he did have an Orthodox Jewish upbringing. But he married out of the faith.

His story is intriguing. He rose to the top of the ranks in

the Confederacy. In fact, the reason he turned down the Supreme Court appointment was he had just been chosen by the
Louisiana legislature to be to Louisiana's Senator. These were
days before the 17th Amendment. So Senators were chosen by
the state legislature, not by direct vote.

And he thought, all things considered, being a senator
was a better job for him. He might have envisioned that if
he'd been on the court it wouldn't be too many years before
he had to resign.

EISNER: So we have a question —

GINSBURG: Oh, I just wanted to say something more about
him: Although he was the leader of the Confederacy, he was a
slaveholder, he was subject to virulent anti-Semitism by others high in the ranks of the Confederacy. They referred to
him as Judas Iscariot.

EISNER: It's true, and I know recently we ran a story about
Confederate monuments because there was so much controversy about them. And there was actually no monument to
him even though he was a leader of the Confederacy. And
it may be just because of what you said—of the way he was
treated among the other Confederate leaders.

GINSBURG: They do have some considerable exhibition about
Benjamin in the museum in New Orleans.

EISNER: And have you seen it?

GINSBURG: Yes.

EISNER: Wow. We have a question from Michael Rosenzweig, a reader in Georgia. He wondered how your Jewishness has affected your life's work as a lawyer, a law professor, a feminist, and a Supreme Court justice.

GINSBURG: Perhaps I should start by saying, I grew up in the shadow of World War II. And we came to know more and more what was happening to the Jews in Europe. The sense of being an outsider—of being one of the people who had suffered oppression for no . . . no sensible reason . . . it's the sense of being part of a minority. It makes you more empathetic to other people who are not insiders, who are outsiders.

I would say that, and love of learning. The sense of being a member of a minority group that somehow has survived generations and generations of hatred and plundering.

But the idea that—think of my own family. My father came from Russia when he was thirteen. He never went to school in any country. He went to a [inaudible] in his shtetl outside Odessa. But—and my mother was the first person in her large family born in the USA. She was born four months after her mother arrived here, so she was conceived in the Old World, born in the New World. And both of them, more than anything else, wanted me to have a good education. That was number one on their list of what I should have.

EISNER: You mentioned growing up in the shadow of World War II and the Holocaust. And I'm wondering if that shaped your views of human rights and human rights law.

GINSBURG: It's certainly a large part of it. I think you probably know that the Holocaust was the beginning of the end of apartheid in America. We were fighting a war against odious racism and our own troops, in that war, until the very end, were rigidly separated by race. So when we were fighting a war against racism, how long could segregation in our own country persist?

So I consider World War II one of the major propelling forces to the *Brown v. Board of Education* decision.

EISNER: So you see a connection between that and then what especially many of those African American soldiers faced coming back to the States, after they had fought and then came back as essentially second class citizens. That's so interesting.

And you feel secure now as a Jew I sense. The beautiful poem that we heard referenced the artwork that's on the walls of your chamber. And there's a mezuzah on the door. I'm just wondering, in your time on the court, how has it accommodated Jewish tradition? Has that changed while you've been there?

GINSBURG: There hadn't been a Jewish justice for some years, from Abe Fortas until my appointment. The clerk of the Supreme Court, Clerk Souter, came to see me very early on in my tenure. And he said, I'm very glad you're here because you can help me with a problem. The Supreme Court admits lawyers to membership in the Supreme Court bar. And every year they would get, oh, a half a dozen or more complaints from Orthodox Jews who said, "we're so proud of our membership in the Supreme Court bar. But we can't frame our certificate included in the wall because it said in the year of our lord so-and-so and he's not our lord." So, I spoke to the chief about this and he said we'll take it up at conference.

And one of my colleagues, and I will not disclose who, said, "In the year of our Lord was good enough for Brandeis, it was good enough for Cardozo, it was good enough for Frankfurter, it was good enough even for Goldberg." And before he got to Fortas, I said, "It's not good enough for Ginsburg."

It took a while for the cycle to complete. First, they said, all right, for the Orthodox Jews we'll have just in the year so-and-so. And then there were some complaints—"We liked what it said on the certificate about the independence of the United States so please keep that on our certificate." Now if you want a certificate showing your membership in the Supreme Court bar you have your choice. You can have just the year 2018. And the year of Our Lord so, or the independence of the United States. It's the way it should be. It's your choice, what you want it to be.

The next was the great Yom Kippur controversy. Usually the High Holy Days come out before the court starts up but sometimes they overlap. So Justice [Stephen] Breyer and I—Justice [Elena] Kagan was not on the court—asked the chief if the court could defer the sitting day. And the first response was, "We confer on Good Friday and nobody complains about that." I said, "I'd be happy to come Thursday that week." Then I think the argument that was utterly convincing for the chief was that inevitably in an argument session there will be Jewish lawyers and you want to put them—this is their day at the Supreme Court. Do you want to take away from them the opportunity to present their case and require them to have a substitute?

And that resonated and so now we don't sit on High Holy Days.

EISNER: Wow. So one of our readers, Jesse Lempell of Cambridge, Massachusetts, had a really interesting question. He noted that you once described an opinion by Israeli justice Aharon Barak that forbid torture even in what they called the ticking time bomb situations—and you said that you thought that opinion had tremendous persuasive value. So I'm wondering as an American Jewish jurist, do you feel any special affinity with the work of the Israeli Supreme Court?

GINSBURG: I feel special affinity to the work of Aharon Barak. He's one of the most brilliant jurists of our time. As you know Israel doesn't have a constitution. But they have five basic laws. And they—the Israeli Supreme Court has a wealth of law to draw on. They have Ottoman Empire law, they have the heritage from the United Kingdom, they have Jewish law. The case that you mentioned—the so-called ticking bomb case—presented to the Israeli Supreme Court this question: the police have apprehended a suspect they believe to know when and where a bomb is going off.

Can we use extreme means—a euphemism for torture—to extract that information? And in a very eloquent judgment written by then-president of the Israeli Supreme Court Barak, the answer was clear. Torture, never. And the opinion explained that there is no greater gift we can give to our enemy than to become so overwhelmed by our concern for security that more and more we come to resemble our enemy in this respect. For human rights.

EISNER: I wonder if we can turn to your personal history for a moment. Your sister, your only sibling, died when she was six and you were less than two years old. Your beloved mother was stricken with cancer during your first year in high school and just sadly died two days before your graduation. I'm just wondering how this affected your sense of wanting to support women and girls. And in particular I understand how much of an inspiration your mother was. I was wondering if you want to tell us a little bit about that.

GINSBURG: My mother was a hugely intelligent woman. She emphasized two things. One was that I should be a lady. And by that she didn't mean fancy dress. What she meant is, be in control of your emotions and don't give way to anger, to remorse, to envy, those emotions just sap strength. And enable you to move forward. And her other message was, be independent.

I suppose she hoped that someday I would meet and marry Prince Charming. Nevertheless, she emphasized the importance of being able to fend for myself.

EISNER: Well and you did marry your Prince Charming right. Marty Ginsburg, your long, longtime partner. But early on in your marriage there was more adversity. He was stricken very sick with cancer. You yourself have battled it twice. And as one of our readers asked, I'm wondering how do you keep going under such challenging circumstances? Where do you draw your strength?

GINSBURG: I think the hardest time was when Marty had testicular cancer. There was no chemotherapy, there was massive surgery and deadly radiation. But we always—we got through each day. And we're thankful that we had and we never thought that he would live as he did.

I was similarly inspired when I had pancreatic cancer by Marilyn Horne who is a great mezzo. And when she was diagnosed with pancreatic cancer, that was her attitude: I will live. And she is still very much alive.

EISNER: Wow, that is amazing. I'd like to turn now to your long and admirable championing of gender equality. I know that you have discussed those early cases in the public before, but I wonder if you might share with our audience tonight just one of your favorite cases? One of the things that you think had the most impact early on in this new field.

GINSBURG: Well, before I answer that question I brought along with me [one of the things that had an impact on me]—there was not too much to inspire young women in my days. There was Nancy Drew and that was just about it. But, I read something by a very young woman. She was barely fifteen when she wrote it. And if I can find it here I'd like to read it to you. So, as I said these are the words of a young woman just turning fifteen.

One of the many questions I have that has so often both-
ered me is why women have been and still are thought to
be so inferior to men. It's easy to say it's unfair. But that's
not good enough for me. I'd like to know the reason for
this great injustice. Men presumably dominated women
from the very beginning because of their greater physical
strength. It's men who earn a living, beget children, and
do as they please. Until recently women silently went
along with this, which was stupid. Since the longer it's
kept up the more deeply entrenched it becomes. Fortunately, education, work, and progress have opened wom-
en's eyes. In many countries they've been granted equal
rights. Many people, mainly women but also men, now
realize how wrong it was to tolerate this state of affairs
for so long.

The letter is signed, Yours, Anne M. Frank.

It was one of the last entries made in her diary. I think
this audience knows she was born in the Netherlands in 1929.
She died in 1945 while imprisoned at Bergen-Belsen just three
months short of her sixteenth birthday.

Isn't that amazing that a child would write that?

EISNER: Yes, I know. I'm so glad that you brought that up
because I think we overlook that aspect of her writing in her
diary.

GINSBURG: Thank you. Well, you asked about gender discrimination litigation.

To pick a favorite is a little like asking me which of my four grandchildren and two step-grandchildren. [*Laughter*]

But I think to illustrate the arbitrariness of gender-based discrimination, Stephen Wiesenfeld's case is as good as any other. And this is Stephen Wiesenfeld's story. He was married to a woman who taught in a public high school. She earned a little more money than he did. She had a healthy pregnancy. She taught into the ninth month.

At the hospital, the doctor came in and told Stephen, you have a healthy baby boy, but your wife died of an embolism. Stephen Wiesenfeld decided at that moment that he would personally care for his infant, that he would not work full-time until the child was in school full-time. So he had heard about something called child-in-care benefits that Social Security afforded. He went down to the local Social Security office. And he said, I'd like to apply for child-in-care benefits. The benefits were arranged so that you could earn up to a certain amount and still get the benefits. Once you went above that amount your benefit was reduced dollar for dollar.

But Stephen thought that with the Social Security benefits and his part time earning he could just about make it. He was told by the attendant at the Social Security office, these are mothers' benefits and not available to fathers. We're in the early '70s now. And Stephen Wiesenfeld writes a letter to the editor of his local Edison, New Jersey newspaper.

It goes like this: "I hear a lot these days about women's lib. Let me tell you my story." And then he recites what happened at the Social Security office and his tagline was, "does Gloria Steinem know about this?"

Well, I was teaching at Rutgers at the time. A woman

who taught on the Spanish faculty lived in the same town, read the letter, and called Stephen Wiesenfeld, suggested that he contact the New Jersey affiliate of the American Civil Liberties Union.

And that's how his case began. The court issued a unanimous judgment but they divided three ways in the rationale. So most of them, led by Justice Brennan, said this is a typical case of the discrimination women encountered. Paula Wiesenfeld paid the same Social Security taxes that the man would pay but her taxes didn't net her family the same benefits that a man's did. And then a few of them thought, this is discrimination against male as parentage. Because the law tells him: you have no choice, you have to be a full-time earner, you have to hire a substitute to yourself to take care of your child.

And then one who later became my chief, then-Justice Rehnquist said, "It's totally arbitrary from the point of view of the baby. Why should the baby have the opportunity for care of a sole surviving parent when the parent who died is male but not when she's female?" So everybody was hurt by this arbitrary gender-based discrimination. That woman is [worth wager] and the male as parent and the baby.

EISNER: I was just saying I feel like there's a lovely metaphor in that sort of triumvirate of answers, in that it shows that gender equality is actually for men and for women and for children. Did you see it that way?

GINSBURG: Very much so and I thought we argued it.

EISNER: Around that time in 1973 you delivered a full

throated support for the Equal Rights Amendment which at that time had passed both houses of Congress but was never ratified by enough states to become part of the Constitution. And I'm just wondering, do we need an ERA now especially in this #MeToo moment?

GINSBURG: First I should say that our Constitution is powerfully hard to amend. And the Congress it takes three-fourths, three-quarters of the states to ratify and the ERA fell three states short. People ask me a question like the one you asked—haven't women progressed under the Fourteenth Amendment's equal protection clause? To get to the point where you would be if they were an Equal Rights Amendment, and my answer is, perhaps.

But then I take out my pocket Constitution and say: I have three granddaughters. I can [take] this Constitution, our fundamental living instrument of government, and point to the First Amendment guaranteeing freedom of speech, press, religion. I would like them to see in that Constitution a statement that men and women are persons of equal citizenship stature. I'd like to see that as a basic tenet of our system. Every constitution in the world written since the year 1950 has an equivalent of an Equal Rights Amendment, a statement that men and women are persons equal in dignity and . . . our Constitution starts out, "We the people, in order to form a more perfect union." And I think part of becoming, a very large part of becoming, a more perfect union is to embrace more and more people. I think about how it was in the beginning, in 1787, when the original Constitution was written.

So, who are we the people? I would not have been there—half the population would not have been there. The people who were held in human bondage, Native Americans, were not part of the political constituency. But over . . . A little over two centuries, I think the genius of the Constitution is that this concept, that this concept of We the People has become ever more embracing. And so I would like to see an Equal Rights Amendment in our Constitution. And I'm still hopeful that there's some movement in Congress to revive the Amendment.

EISNER: You have spoken recently about your own #MeToo moment, which happened years ago. And one of our readers wondered whether you still experience sexism today?

GINSBURG: Not that kind of sexism! I'm soon going to be eighty-five. But is there a lingering bias? I think in the decade of the '70s most of the explicit gender-based classification were gone, a combination of legislatures changing, courts issuing decisions. It was a conversation between the courts and the legislature to accomplish that change. Getting rid of almost all of the explicit gender-based lines.

What's left is what has been called unconscious bias. And my best example of that is the symphony orchestra. When I was growing up, I never saw a woman in the symphony orchestra except perhaps the harpist.

Howard Taubman, who is a well-known music critic for the *New York Times*, said that he could tell whether it's a woman playing on the piano, the violin. One day someone decided to put him to the test so they sat him down and they blindfolded him. Then they had a procession of young artists come out and perform.

And he was all mixed up. He got it all wrong. So then

someone came up with the brilliant idea: let's drop a curtain. So that the judges of the competition would not see the people who were auditioning. And with that almost overnight there was a change in the composition of symphony orchestras.

A young violinist, when I told this story at a music festival some years ago, said, "Well, you left out something." "What did I leave out?" "You have to have that we auditioned shoeless. They wouldn't let a woman's heels come in."

Now unfortunately we can't replicate the dropped curtain in every area. There's a wonderful slim volume that's two lectures by Mary Beard in which she explains . . . The first one is about women's voicelessness. And the second is women in power.

But she starts with the story of Penelope coming down to where the suitors are and Telemachus her son telling her, mother, you're not supposed to speak in public. Women don't speak in public.

EISNER: This is in Homer's *Odyssey*.

GINSBURG: Yes. I don't know how many times I attended meetings as young faculty member where I would say something and there was silence and the discussion went on. And then maybe ten, fifteen minutes later a man would say just what I had [and there] would be reaction. The idea.

There was a tendency to tune out when a woman was speaking because you couldn't expect her to say anything worthwhile.

EISNER: Well, in fact this condition really might be

continuing. I found a study in 2015 of the women Supreme Court justices, so that would be you and Justices Kagan and Sotomayor—that you were interrupted three times more often than your male colleagues.

Now this was an academic study. Does that ring true to you? Does it mean anything?

GINSBURG: I think the academic study is accurate if you look at the transcripts. I'm glad that that report came out because I think things will change, men will be more conscious that this is happening. On the other side I did say that we have been so good about not interrupting. When Justice Scalia was alive it was a competition between Sotomayor and Scalia to see who could ask the most questions in an oral argument.

So many . . .

Let me tell you. It's very Jewish story. So . . . one day in an argument session Justice O'Connor was asked a question. And then I jumped in. And she said, "Just a minute, I'm not finished." Next day in *USA Today*, headline, "Rude Ruth interrupts Sandra."

At lunch immediately after the argument, I apologize and she said, really, don't worry about it at all. The guys do it to each other all the time. So when I was asked my reaction to this article, that's what my response was. The reporter who wrote this story watched for the next two arguments. He said, "She's right. I never noticed it when the men are interrupting each other."

Then a woman came to my rescue from Georgetown— a great expert in language—and she tried to explain how was it that I came to interrupt Sandra. Well, Justice Sandra

Day O'Connor is from a ranch on the border between New Mexico and Arizona, a laid-back gal from the West. And I am a fast-talking Jewish girl from New York. When people who know the two of us know that Sandra got two words for my every word. But that's a very typical, meant well, illustration that Jews are fast talking and susceptible to interrupting each other.

EISNER: So many of our readers—men and especially women—are really hungry for your advice. Here's Becky from Raleigh, North Carolina. She says she has been working as a paralegal for only a few months and has already faced discrimination. She wants to pursue her dream of a legal career. What advice would you give her?

GINSBURG: First, find allies. Being a loner is hard, but if you have other people with you that points to your confidence and your spirit. And don't respond to an insult you have experienced by saying "you sexist pig."

I thought that my job in the early '70s was to be a kind of a kindergarten teacher, to explain to justices that there really was a thing as gender-based discrimination.

There was a big difference between their understanding of racial discrimination and gender discrimination. Racial discrimination was odious. Discrimination between men and women, the myth was that it always operates benignly in the woman's favor. So to tell a man who thinks he's been a very good husband and a very good father that he is a discriminator, it takes an education for them to see that there really is such a thing, because every time the Supreme Court met up with a gender-based classification before 1971 it rationalized it as a favor to women. Women weren't put on the jury roles. "Well, that's a favor: they mustn't be distracted from their work as the center of home and family life."

Never mind that it has something to say about women's citizenship. Citizens have obligations as well as rights. One obligation is to participate in the justice system. Men are obliged to serve but women are expendable. Or the notion that . . . one typical law passed by the state of Michigan in the 1940s: a woman could not serve as a bartender unless her husband or her father owned the establishment. The testing case was a mother owned a tavern and her daughter was her bartender. The Supreme Court dispatched that as legislation meant to protect the woman from unsavory places. Never mind that there was no restriction on the woman being a barmaid—that is the one who carried the drinks to the table. She didn't stand behind a bar to protect her.

That was in 1943 . . . but that was the thinking with these classifications. It took a while for judges to understand what Justice Brennan said so well: This pedestal that women are supposed to stand on more often than turns out to be a cage. So that was mission to get judges to understand that there really such a thing as gender-based discrimination.

EISNER: So one of the justices that it seems you've had over the years the warmest and most unusual relationship [with] is the late Justice Antonin Scalia. And there are many people who marvel at the fact that the two of you disagreed so vehemently and yet had such a warm and deep relationship, and some of our readers asked about this. A teacher wrote in and said her public policy students say they can't talk to their peers whose political views differ from their own. Another reader says it's so hard to talk to family members these days and friends who don't agree with them. So I'm wondering, how did you and Justice Scalia do it?

GINSBURG: The first time I met Justice Scalia he was then a professor teaching at the University of Chicago. I attended a lecture he gave. I disagree with a lot of what he said but I was totally captivated by the way he said it.

He is a man—was a man—with a great sense of humor. When we became buddies on the D.C. Circuit, where the court sits in panels of three judges, and he would whisper something to me in the middle of an oral argument it would totally crack me up. All I can do to avoid bursting out in hilarious laughter.

We shared certain things. One is he was brought up in Queens. I was brought up in Brooklyn in roughly similar neighborhoods where people were either Irish or Italian or Jewish. We both really cared about families. We had an annual New Year's party where the fare would be whatever, you know, hunted. So usually it was Bambi and my husband, who was a great chef, made venison. And whatever children were around came. And then we shared a love of opera. In fact there is an opera, it was a comic opera, called "Scalia-Ginsburg."

And I think it does a wonderful job of explaining our friendship. It starts out with Scalia's rage aria. And the rage is typical Handelian in style. It goes like this: The justices are blind/How can they possibly spout this/The Constitution says absolutely nothing. About this. And then I respond that he is searching for [bright line] solutions to problems that don't have easy answers. But, the great thing about our Constitution is that like our society, it can evolve.

Well then Scalia gets locked up in a dark room. He's being punished for excessive dissenting. And he has to go through certain tests to get out.

So I enter through a ceiling.

And then I tell the character of Don Giovanni who's in this, Scalia Ginsburg, was called the Commendatore. And he is astonished: he said, "Why would you want to help him? He's your enemy." And then we do a wonderful duet.

I say, "He's not my enemy, he's my dear friend. Yes, we are different but we are one—different in the way we approach interpretation of legal texts. But one in our reverence for the Constitution and for the institution we serve."

We recently had excerpts from the opera "Scalia-Ginsburg" at the Library of Congress. The audience were members and staff of the House and Senate Judiciary Committee.

The next day Senator Grassley asked if he could have a copy of my remarks.

Sometimes I would speak to Justice Scalia in private and say, "This is so over the top, what you have written. Tone it down, it will be more persuasive." He never took that advice.

But on the other hand he would come into my chambers. Scalia was a great grammarian. His father was a Latin teacher at Brooklyn College and his mother had been a grade school teacher, so if I made a grammatical error he would let

me know. He'd either call or come into chambers. He never
sent a message, never sent a memo around so that I could be
embarrassed at the mistakes I made.

EISNER: Do you think that there are lessons in your friendship now? We're in such a polarized time and I think people
really are thirsty for role models that are able to transcend
their philosophical or political or judicial differences. Is there
any lesson in your friendship for us?

GINSBURG: Well I think it is our caring about the welfare,
the good and welfare of the court. And anybody who is in a
decision-making body, that should be number one priority. I
would say that the Supreme Court is the most collegial place
I've ever worked, beyond any law faculty, beyond the D.C.
Circuit. We all respect and in most cases genuinely like each
other.

EISNER: And I probably can't ask you to describe . . .

GINSBURG: But let me tell you the way it was in the not
so good old days. Think of Justice Brandeis coming on the
court. He is a second Wilson appointee. The first was Justice McReynolds. Justice McReynolds was an out-and-out
anti-Semite. And when Brandeis, this brilliant man who was
sometimes called Isaiah, when Brandeis got up to speak in
conference, McReynolds would leave the room. Really.

EISNER: Did anyone object, did anyone say this is wrong?

GINSBURG: Yes, in time he overcame his difficulties.

EISNER: So you had a very warm and loving and quite un-usual partnership with your late husband Marty. I understand that he was much more socially gregarious than you were for many years. He was a great cook. And a raconteur. And it does seem that since his passing your public persona has grown, and I'm wondering if that's a coincidence or whether there is some connection there.

GINSBURG: Marty was my biggest booster all my life. We were married the same month I graduated from college. Marty had his first year of law school. He was then taken out at the tail end of the Korean War for service. So when he went back, he was in his second year, I was in my first year. And one of his classmates, this is someone I had known at Cornell, said to me, "You know your husband, he's bragging about you. He's saying you're going to be on the law review—and I looked at you and you were this little twerp person."

But that's the way Marty was—always made me feel I was a little bit better than I thought I was. But which was extraordinary for a young man. In the '50s I went to a school, Cornell University, where the ratio was four men to every woman, it was the ideal place for parents of a daughter.

If you could not find a man at Cornell you were hopeless.

What made Marty so overwhelmingly attractive to me is that he cared that I had a brain and I hadn't met a guy be-fore who was interested at all. And some of my classmates at Cornell, very bright women, they would play dumb. That was the way to please the man, to make him feel more important. Marty was so secure in his own ability that he never regarded me with any kind of a threat. Far from it. I think his idea was, if I decided I wanted to spend the rest of my life with Ruth she's gotta be something special.

EISNER: Yes, it's rather hard to imagine you playing dumb. So you're rather famous person now, you know, and I'm just wondering, I mean, here you have your own swag and there's mugs and you have your tote bag—your dissent tote bag. Is it strange to see your face on mugs and tote bags?

GINSBURG: Well this is all the creation of a second-year law student . . . [inaudible] and it started when the Supreme Court decided the Shelby County case that cut the heart out of the Voting Rights Act of 1965. [inaudible] was angry about what the court did and then decided that anger is a useless emotion she would do something affirmative, something positive. So she created this Tumblr that starts with my dissent in Shelby County case.

And then she thought about its proper name. Someone suggested a fellow Brooklynite. The Notorious BIG. People didn't know that we had that very important thing in common. And it's just taken off from there. I mean it's amazing to me. In March I will be eighty-five, and everyone wants to take my picture.

EISNER: So Kate McKinnon plays you on *Saturday Night Live*, Felicity Jones is starring as you in a new feature film, a documentary just debuted last week at Sundance. How does it feel to see yourself on the screen?

GINSBURG: I've seen the documentary, it's really good. It's really good.

Kathleen Peratis, who introduced me, is in it. My personal trainer is in it. The filmmakers spent an hour in the gym with the two of us and maybe two, three minutes shows in the film. The one with Felicity Jones . . . I should give equal billing to the person who plays Marty—Marty is Armie Hammer. And so somebody said, for one he's taller than Marty. They said, and do you think you're the same height as Felicity Jones? Anyway that film was called *On the Basis of Sex*. And it will be up probably at the end of 2018.

The script was written by my nephew, the son of Marty's sister, and he based it on a case that Marty and I had argued together. It is a case that didn't go to the Supreme Court and I asked Daniel my nephew why he had picked that case, and he said because he wanted this film to be as much about a marriage as it was about the legal case. And the case is very good. It's Charles E. Moritz versus the Commissioner of Internal Revenue. This was a man who took good care of his mother though she was ninety-three. The Internal Revenue Code had a deduction. If you hired someone to be a substitute for yourself to take care of a child, an elderly parent and infirm relative to any age. The deduction was available to any woman. Or to a widowed divorced man. Charles E. Moritz never married. He took that deduction. It was disallowed. He filed his own case in tax court. He filed his own brief which was the soul of simplicity. It said, "If I were a dutiful daughter I would have gotten this deduction. I'm a dutiful son. What sense does this make?"

I think the tax court judge said something to the effect of, "We glean the taxpayer is making a constitutional argument. But everyone knows that the Internal Revenue code is immune from constitutional attack. It's riddled with arbitrary lines."

Anyway we took Charles E. Moritz's case to the 10th Circuit in Denver. The 10th Circuit decided that case in our favor. Congress changed the law retrospectively, that was the interplay between the court and the legislature. The court said this standard line is no good and the legislature fixed it. Nevertheless the solicitor general asked the Supreme Court to review the decision. And explain that even though this gender line was over, the 10th Circuit's decision casts a cloud of unconstitutionality over dozens of federal statutes. See Appendix E. Appendix E was a list of every provision in the U.S. Code that differentiated on the basis of gender. It came from the Department of Defense computer—these were the days when no one had a personal computer—but it was a bonanza. There it was, all the provisions that needed to be changed.

So that is the case that is the center of, *On the Basis of Sex*. That's the name of the film.

EISNER: So many democratic norms seem to be under assault now, undermined. The media, the judiciary, I'm just wondering if you think there is a moment when justices should respond.

GINSBURG: The judiciary is a reactive branch of government. It doesn't generate the controversies that come before it. It has no agenda. It's reactive to what's out there. A very fine federal judge, Judge Goldberg from the Fifth Circuit, once said, "The court don't make conflagrations but they do their best to put them out." If people ask me about an opinion all I can say is that judges do depend on the bar to explain the importance of an independent judiciary. It is our nation's hallmark and pride. The federal judiciary.

EISNER: Are there any decisions that you regret?

GINSBURG: I can answer that question by telling you the advice I was given when I was a brand-new judge on the D.C. Circuit by my senior colleague Ed Tam. He said "Ruthie, you've got to work hard on every case. Every opinion you write. But when it's released, when it's over, don't look back. Don't waste your time worrying about what's done. Go on to the next case and give it your all." And that is wonderful advice for judge.

EISNER: And were you able to follow that with that?

GINSBURG: Without any difficulty, yes.

EISNER: I am really impressed.

GINSBURG: My, I must say, I haven't had the kind of challenge that some of my colleagues had when asked about *Bush v. Gore.* So Justice Scalia's answer to people, he says, "Get over it."

EISNER: So over the years there's been a suggestion that the lifetime tenure of Supreme Court justices be replaced by a set term. That might, say, span several presidencies. It might reduce partisan anxiety. It could mean that older judges could be selected to serve. It could be a graceful way for judges perhaps past their prime to leave the bench.

And I'm just wondering what you think about this idea.

GINSBURG: It is a subject on which I am biased and prejudiced. And I will admit, most countries in the world have a compulsory retirement age. Most of our states have compulsory retirement age for judges. Some have a fixed term, fixed non-renewable term, but I'm grateful to the founding fathers for writing into the Constitution that the judges shall hold their office during good behavior. So, many people have asked me well, when are you going to step down.

AUDIENCE: Never!

GINSBURG: My first response was, I had a painting on loan from the Museum of American art by Josef Albers and I loved it. And he took it away from me for a traveling show. About eight years later it came back. So I said I couldn't even begin to think about me until I get my Albers back.

Now the next was Brandeis. He was the same age as I was when he was appointed. He stepped down after twenty-three-years. But now I'm the longest sitting Jewish justice—more than Brandeis, more than Frankfurter. So I can't use that.

So I'm just candid and say as long as I can do the job full steam I will be here.

EISNER: We are sadly almost out of time. There is one

question that I must ask you. If I can take a personal privilege here it's a question that I had the privilege of asking President Obama and Prime Minister Benjamin Netanyahu and Susan Rice when she was national security adviser. What is your favorite flavor of bagel?

GINSBURG: A New York poppyseed bagel.

EISNER: This is amazing! I did not know the answer to this and this may be the only thing that Barack Obama and Benjamin Netanyahu and Ruth Bader Ginsburg agree on. They all pick poppyseed. Wow. I am amazed.

So of all the many questions and notes from readers that we received one stands out and I'd like to quote from this in our closing. It comes from Carly Rae Brown of Evansville, Indiana and Carly, I hope that you are watching. She is nine years old in the fourth grade and she says that she is your biggest fan. Her Girl Scout troop marched in a Christmas parade and they were asked to hold up signs about what they wanted to be when they grew up and her sign said Supreme Court Justice. And she wants to be a Justice, she says, to support women's rights and other people who aren't treated fairly. She also—are you ready—wants to be called C.R.B.

And here's her question. She said, "What can I do now as a nine-year-old to make a change. How can I follow in your footsteps?"

GINSBURG: May I say first that the idea of a young girl aspiring to be a judge, even more, even more Supreme Court justice is a wonderful thing. I have a granddaughter who is now a lawyer. When she was eight I was being filmed for some show. My granddaughter Clara was with me and she said she wanted to be in the film too. So the maker said, "Oh all right Clara, we'll ask you a question. What would you like to be when you grow up?" And this then eight-year-old said "I would like to be president of the United States of the world."

It's the difference between the aspirations that young women can have today and what they had in the so-called good old days. I think she should take her schoolwork very seriously and become a good reader. Reading is tremendously important in the job now. And then do things in your community—I'm sure you will find things. Whether it's assisting in getting food to the homeless people or if you care about the environment, helping keep local parks clean. And anything that you can do to make things a little better in your community. So that is what I would advise her to do.

EISNER: Well she asked me to ask you to please stay on the Supreme Court until she can take your spot.

Somehow I think there are people in this room who might agree.

I just want to thank you all. This has just been an amazing evening. Personal thanks to my dear friend and wonderful supporter Kathleen Peratis for the lovely introduction and for all that you did to make this happen. To Rabbi Holtzblatt and Rabbi Alexander as well as David Polonsky and Courtney Tisch, all the people of Adas Israel, you guys are amazing. it was such a pleasure to work with you. I'd like to recognize the Forward's board chair Jake Morowitz and our president Sam Norich. And the rest of the *Forward*'s national board, many of whom flew in here to Washington to be here tonight. And *Forward* readers and supporters. Without your generous support, we couldn't do what we can do and for all of you who came here tonight and all of those who are watching on webcasts and Facebook online. Thank you so much for being part of this wonderful conversation.

And of course our greatest thanks to Justice Ruth Bader Ginsburg.

THE LAST INTERVIEW: BILL MOYERS IN CONVERSATION WITH RUTH BADER GINSBURG

INTERVIEW BY BILL MOYERS
MOYERS ON DEMOCRACY
UNION THEOLOGICAL SEMINARY, NEW YORK CITY
FEBRUARY 12, 2020

Every year the Judith Davidson Moyers Women of Spirit Award Lecture brings an outstanding woman to meet with students, faculty and friends of Union Theological Seminary in New York City.

This year's guest was Supreme Court Justice Ruth Bader Ginsburg.

A Supreme Court Justice for twenty-seven years now, "The Notorious RBG" has also become a cultural icon who regularly attracts huge crowds to her public appearances. They packed the house at Union where she was interviewed by journalist Bill Moyers.

BILL MOYERS: Welcome indeed. As you can see, Justice Ginsburg, it's a full house here to greet you. The chapel is packed with Union faculty, staff, administration, friends. Guests have come from the Jewish Theological Seminary across the way, and from the religion departments of Barnard and Columbia, your law school alma mater. Still more in the balcony yonder, and in a room you and I can't see, the overflowing room, it's overflowing. And many are joining us by streaming. So the Union community has gathered and we thank you very much for coming.

First, a personal note. Two weeks ago, Judith and I were at the Library of Congress. The LBJ Foundation was presenting the Justice with its annual Liberty and Justice Award for All. And they had asked me to do a brief tribute to the

Justice, so I spent weeks plunging into her work. The books about her. The biography. Biographies. The most recent and excellent book called *Conversations with RBG*, which is just out and is a terrific book.

And especially her briefs. I have read briefs in my life, but never as many briefs as I have read in the last three months. And what I discovered in both the dissenting briefs and the affirming briefs is a remarkable style, a remarkable body of prose that is lean and muscular as if it'd been in with a first rate trainer for the last thirty years. And that was picturesque and descriptive and insightful. I never enjoyed reading anything legal as much as I did those briefs.

And then I discovered a little-known fact about her. Maybe some of you do who know her well personally. But she had studied European literature at Cornell in the '50s with Vladimir Nabokov. And he had obviously had, reportedly had, and substantially had an impact on this unusual, remarkable, visible and particular prose.

So in your spare time, I urge you to get those briefs, I'm going to mention a few of them a little later, and read them. They are remarkable literature. So I want to begin by asking you, Justice Ginsburg, what did you take away from that time with Nabokov that you feel definitely shifted your way of writing?

JUSTICE RUTH BADER GINSBURG: We called him Nabokov, the various pronunciations. He was a man who was in love with the sound of words. I think English was his third language. His first language was French and then Russian. And he explained why he liked writing in English better than other languages.

And he gave his example. The white horse. Well, if you say it in French, it's *le cheval blanc*. But when you say *cheval*, you see a brown horse. You have to adjust your image to make it white. But because we put the adjective first, when the horse comes, it's already white.

MOYERS: Is it true that he influenced your using the phrase "gender discrimination" instead of "sex discrimination," and that you made the change?

GINSBURG: That change was brought about by my secretary at Columbia Law School. Millicent Tryan was her name. She said to me one day, "I've been typing these briefs and audibles for you, and the word sex juts out all over. Don't you know that the men you are addressing"—because the federal bench was then virtually all male—"don't you know that their first association with the word sex is not what you want to be on their minds."

"So choose a gender-neutral word, a grammar book term, and that will ward off distracting associations." So I thought that she was so right, and I began to use "gender-based discrimination." And the court picked it up too. So now you will see gender used.

MOYERS: Did you ever think of giving up law for a novel? Did you ever think of becoming a novelist after that experience?

GINSBURG: I loved the law. I loved the study of law. Unlike many law students, I thoroughly enjoyed my three years in law school. I don't think I have the capacity to be a good novelist. But in the trade, I have been in—for goodness knows how many years—it's hard to believe I've been on the Supreme Court for twenty-seven years.

MOYERS: Right. Do you have in your head how many briefs you have written?

GINSBURG: How many opinions?

MOYERS: Yes, opinions.

GINSBURG: Hundreds and hundreds, because before I was on the Supreme Court I was for thirteen years on the Court of Appeals for the D.C. circuit. In those thirteen years I wrote hundreds of opinions, and on the Supreme Court, I don't have an accurate count of them, but there is a record of how many, and they're in the hundreds.

There's an opinion of the court in every case, but then every justice is free to write separately either a concurring opinion, joining in on the majority's judgment, but for different reasons, or a dissenting opinion. And you perhaps noticed a difference between an opinion that speaks for the court.

At our conferences I'll take careful notes of what my colleagues thought about a case, and if I am assigned the opinion, I will try to incorporate other views, because I'm writing for the court. But if I'm writing a dissent, I don't have to worry about what the others—

MOYERS: Right.

GINSBURG: —thought. I have a free hand.

MOYERS: Well, if you had become a novelist, we'd have missed some marvelous opinions, and I'm so glad I had that chance to read them. But it takes me back to the question why did you become a lawyer?

GINSBURG: Goes back to my undergraduate days at Cornell University. It was not a great time for our country. It was the heyday of Senator Joseph McCarthy from Wisconsin. There was a tremendous red scare in the country. There was the House Un-American Activities Committee and the Senate's comparable investigating committee, calling people, many of them in the entertainment business, or writers, having them come before Congress to try to justify why they had belonged to a pink-tinged organization in their youth in the 1930s, at height of the Depression.

I had a great professor for constitutional law at Cornell. His name was Robert E. Cushman. And he wanted me to be aware that our country was straying from its most basic values. That is the right to think, speak and write as you believe. And not as a Big Brother government tells you is the right way to think, speak and write.

And he made me aware that there were lawyers standing up for these people, reminding our Congress that we had a First Amendment that guarantees freedom of expression. We have a Fifth Amendment protecting us against self-incrimination.

I drew from that that being a lawyer was a pretty nifty thing to be, because you could earn a living, but you could also do things for which you were not paid that would make conditions a little better in your community. So it was that idea of a lawyer is more than someone who works for a day's pay, but someone who has a skill that can help make things a little better.

MOYERS: There runs through your life and your work a deep moral thread. A moral imperative. Where does that come from?

GINSBURG: Where did it? I don't know in particular where you drew that from, but I have often quoted an expression that Martin Luther King was fond of, and that is that the arc of the moral universe is long, but it bends towards justice. And I believe that fervently.

I've seen it in my own lifetime. Things may not be now as we would like them to be, but think of how far we have come. For example, I grew up when World War II was raging, and we were fighting a war against odious racism. And yet, our own troops, until the very end of the war, were rigidly separated—

MOYERS: Right.

GINSBURG: —by race. That was wrong, and I think World War II was a major contributor to the Supreme Court eventually ending apartheid in America, with the *Brown v. Board* decision.

MOYERS: 1954, I believe.

GINSBURG: Yes.

MOYERS: Yes.

GINSBURG: In '54. But you think of the way things were, the racial injustice that existed in our country, the confined opportunities open to women. It was the closed-door era for women, and I have seen those doors open wide. I've seen what was once the closed door replaced by a welcome mat. So I am an optimist, because I know that there is the possibility of change if people really care to make it happen.

And that's important, because I never could have done what I did if there hadn't been a groundswell among women in the late '60s and throughout the '70s, wanting to tear down the barriers. Wanting to free both women and men to be you and me. To follow your own talents—

MOYERS: Right.

GINSBURG: —as far as it could take you.

MOYERS: When I ask you that question about that moral imperative, I thought you were perhaps going to come back with something about the Hebrew prophets. And I did my graduate work in theology and church history, and the only courses I came close to flunking were two years of Hebrew. If I hadn't been married to Judith I would never have come out of it.

But I did spend enough time with that to think I heard, in some of your opinions, that cadence of the prophet. That outrage that comes with the sight of injustice. And I found where you said, after you took the oath at the Supreme Court, "I am a judge born, raised, and proud of being a Jew. The demand for justice runs through the entirety of the Jewish tradition. I hope in my years on the bench of the Supreme Court of the United States I will have the strength and courage to remain constant in the service of that demand." When I read that, I realized that explains the Biblical command on the wall that—

GINSBURG: Justice, justice—

MOYERS: —was in your chamber. Is it still in your chamber?

GINSBURG: It's from Deuteronomy. And it says, "Justice, justice shall thou pursue, that thou may thrive." Yes. And also what I came away with from my Jewish heritage is a love of learning. Learning is highly prized among Jews. My father came here from Russia when he was thirteen. He went to night school to learn English. He never had any formal education except Hebrew school in any country.

My mother was the first child in her large family to be born in the USA. Education was tremendously important to them. And I grew up learning to love to read. My fondest memories as a child were sitting on my mother's lap while she read to me. So yes, it's the opposition to injustice and wanting to do something about it. There's a Jewish expression about the obligation to help repair tears in the society in which we live.

MOYERS: I came upon an editorial you wrote in your high school paper, I believe, in which you did an amazing account of the importance of the Magna Carta. Or the ten commandments first. The Magna Carta, the 1681 or '91—

GINSBURG: Bill of Rights.

MOYERS: —Bill of Rights in England, the Declaration of Independence, which marked the framework for a new government, and the UN charter that was adopted—

GINSBURG: Yes.

MOYERS: —and how did you at that age bring those documents together in what's a brief but remarkable exposition?

GINSBURG: It was in the eighth grade. World War II had just ended and there was great optimism. There was an organization with a name something like the World Federalists. Everyone was hoping for this one world that would live at peace, and that the rule of law would take over.

It hasn't worked out quite as well as the expectation at the time, but it was very, very hopeful time. And the UN charter was the ideal one world. At peace. Was alive. It didn't take too long before the Iron Curtain came down and we began what endured for so many years.

MOYERS: But you were optimistic, despite the fact that you were born in the midst of the Depression. You were born in '33.

GINSBURG: Yes.

MOYERS: I was born in '34. Judith was born in '35. So we've got between us 250-some odd years. And it was after the Depression and after World War II. I think both us were quite optimistic then, even though we were too young to know what optimism was. But we were hopeful about the future.

But something else—I almost brought it tonight and I thought it would take too long. So that was in the eighth grade. Was it in high school then you came upon that writing by Anne Frank in which she—and I'd never seen this before. I read her diary. Seen the documentaries. But she talks about the plight of women.

GINSBURG: Yes.

MOYERS: And why women are taking the subordination to men. She said it's stupid.

GINSBURG: Yes.

MOYERS: She says, "It's stupid." And she says, "I can only explain it by the fact that, well, men are more physical, men do the work and men can do as they please," or something like that. And then she says, "I just hope women will wake up one day and realize what's been done to them, and do something about it."

GINSBURG: Yes. And she was fifteen years old.

MOYERS: Fifteen years old. Where did you find that?

GINSBURG: It's in the diary toward the end. It was one of the last entries before she was sent off to I think Bergen-Belsen, where she died, I think about a month short of her sixteenth birthday.

MOYERS: Can you remember what you thought when you read that about women in Anne Frank's diary?

GINSBURG: I don't remember the first time I encountered it, because I read the diaries a few times. But it was a real eye-opener. I knew that these situations, these conditions existed, but I thought, "Well, that's just the way it is. There's not much you can do about it. You'll have to cope with it." But that's a remarkable entry in her diary.

MOYERS: Right.

GINSBURG: And she mentioned some progress too. She said, "In some countries they've been given equal rights."

MOYERS: Things were better. Right. For women. Who were your role models when you were a young girl? I know one was your mother, Celia.

GINSBURG: I had a fictional role model and a real one. You're right that my mother was a constant encourager, telling me, "Be independent, whatever else you do. It would be nice if you met and married Prince Charming, but be prepared to fend for yourself."

The fictional heroine was Nancy Drew, because most books for children at that time were of the Jane and Jack variety, where Jack was running and doing all kinds of fun things, and Jane or Jill was sitting in a pretty pink party dress. But Nancy Drew was a doer. She was leading around her boyfriend. She had adventures. She solved mysteries.

The real woman who was a heroine for me was Amelia Earhart. I can't say that I had women judges as a model, except for Deborah in the Bible, because women weren't on the bench. I mean even when I started law school women were only 3 percent of the lawyers across the country. I think young women today have many women who inspire them. There's no closed doors for women anymore. Women can be admirals. They can be chief judges. So it was Nancy Drew and Amelia Earhart.

MOYERS: What about the Greek deities?

GINSBURG: Oh yes. My mother took me on weekly trips to the library. And while she got her hair done, I would pick out the five books I'd take home. And Greek mythology I loved. My closest friend growing up was Catholic, and she had all these saints and I had nothing but this one God. So that's when I became a lover of Greek mythology.

MOYERS: Athena in particular, I believe.

GINSBURG: Oh, Pallas Athena, who gave her father a headache.

MOYERS: She is said to have been—I was struck by this when

I came across it, because when I was about that age, growing up in a small town in east Texas, walking down East Burleson Street. They had just opened the new, small library built by the Business and Professional Women there, our first real external library outside of the courthouse.

And I went in and I picked out two books to take home. First books that I'd ever had. One was Jules Verne's *Around the World in 80 Days*, and the other was a book of Greek heroes. And about the same time you were reading about Athena, I was reading about the males who were often the object of their wrath.

So we have that in common. That framed an issue with me. Jules Verne enhanced my desire to be a journalist, because he'd travel the world and did it on somebody else's expense account. And I liked that. But Athena was said to have established the rule of law when she—

GINSBURG: Yes.

MOYERS: —tried Orestes? Right?

GINSBURG: Yes.

MOYERS: For the murder of her—for the murder of her mother, who had killed his father.

GINSBURG: Yes.

MOYERS: And so she was said to have put down the first frame for the rule of justice.

GINSBURG: Yes.

MOYERS: And I wondered if you saw something in the future for you because of that?

GINSBURG: I did not dream—

MOYERS: Okay.

GINSBURG: —of being a judge. Of course there may have been Athena, but she was immortal. And there was no mortal. In fact, it wasn't until Jimmy Carter became president that women showed up on the federal bench in numbers. Go back to when I was in law school, there had been just one woman in the entire history of the country who had ever served on a federal appellate bench. She was Florence Allen from Ohio. She retired in 1959, the year I graduated from law school, and there were none again until Johnson. Johnson appointed Shirley Hufstedler—

MOYERS: That's right.

GINSBURG: —to the Ninth Circuit. And then Carter made Shirley Hufstedler the first ever secretary of education. There were none again. Carter thought, "I've seen these federal judges. They all look just like me. But that's not how the great United States looks."

So he was determined to appoint members of minority groups and women in numbers to the federal bench. There was no vacancy on the Supreme Court. He had only four years in office, but he transformed the federal judiciary. He named I think over twenty-five women to district court, trial court benches, and then eleven to courts of appeals. And I was one of the lucky eleven.

Then President Reagan takes office and he doesn't want to be outdone. So he is determined to put the first woman on the Supreme Court. He made a nationwide search and came up with a brilliant choice in Sandra Day O'Connor. And no president has gone back to the not so good old days. So women are now something, like, close to a third of the federal bench. Not enough, but it's certainly moved in the right—

MOYERS: Right.

GINSBURG: —direction.

MOYERS: Let me take half a step back, and then we're going to move to some matters of law. That you grew up in Flatbush, in Brooklyn. Flatbush at one time it was one of the original Brooklyn colonies in the old days, and then it became, by the time you came along, the largest concentration of urban Jewish people in the world, believe it or not.

Mixing it up with the Irish, the Poles, the Italians and some Syrians. And there is, in your biography and other accounts of Flatbush in the '30s and '40s, a sense of energy and drive. And, you know, some conflict, obviously, when that many people are aspiring for their daily bread.

But you lived near Coney Island and you could see across the way, I'm told, the Statue of Liberty. There was something that one writer called a thorough Americanness about Flatbush. Did you sense that? Did you get the patriotic vibrations and the jostling that was taking place in the country around that time?

GINSBURG: Most of the people in my neighborhood, their parents came from the old world. Certainly no further back than their grandparents. Our neighborhood, as many in New York, was about evenly divided among Jews, Italians and Irish. And then, as you said, there was a smattering of other.

What there wasn't in our neighborhood were African Americans. And even when I went to law school, I think it was mentioned that I was one of nine women in a class of over 500. In that same class with nine women, there's only one African American in the entire Harvard Law School first year class.

MOYERS: Just one?

GINSBURG: Just one.

MOYERS: Well, I lived in a small town in Texas. Grew up 20,000 people, 10,000 black and 10,000 white. And rarely did the twain interact. We saw each other from a distance, but it proved, as I've said many times, that you could grow up well loved, well taught and well churched and still not know anything about the lived experience of someone else just across the tracks, right?

GINSBURG: And you might know of a case named *Sweatt v. Painter*. Texas finally realized it couldn't exclude African

Americans from legal education. So it set up, I think in the '40s, a separate school. Separate and vastly unequal. That decision, *Sweatt v. Painter*, was one of the building blocks leading to *Brown v. Board*.

Because the Supreme Court said, "Without overturning *Plessy v. Ferguson* that introduced the separate but equal notion, these schools are vastly unequal. African Americans cannot be kept out of the University of Texas Law School."

So, I was living in Brooklyn when Branch Rickey hired Jackie Robinson to be on the Dodgers, and that was such an exciting time. We had no idea of what this man was exposed to. Not only from other teams, but his own teammates.

I have a passion for opera. You never saw an African American on an opera stage. There was Marion Anderson, great contralto. She wasn't allowed to sing in D.C. in Constitution Hall. Finally the Met engaged her when she was well past her prime. So although we were a melting pot of people from Europe, both Eastern and West, African Americans did not live in the same neighborhoods.

MOYERS: Well, I cheered your opinion in I think it was *Fisher v. the University of Texas*—

GINSBURG: Yes.

MOYERS: —because it was an affirmative action case, and we in the Johnson administration had pushed affirmative action until we got a significant backlash. But LBJ made one of the greatest speeches of his time in politics at Howard University, when he said, "How can we say that if we untie people who've been running with their feet tied and bring them to the start-ing line, they can keep up with everybody else who has never been tied."

And in *Fisher v. the University of Texas*, I believe, cor-rect me if I'm wrong, you wrote—and that's our university, Judith and mine. You wrote that if a university wants to adopt a modest or moderate affirmative action program, why not? I love the way you phrase it, as if it were just a natural thing, not some great mountain that had been moved. You remem-ber that?

GINSBURG: Yes. Yes.

MOYERS: It had a big impact, of course, in Texas. Well, starting with the cauldron where you grew up and your idol, your heroes and your reading and your parents, and your ex-perience at Cornell, I want to take you to the Voting Rights Act that I have mentioned and Judith mentioned in her in-troduction.

I was there in the White House with LBJ when he signed the Voting Rights Act in 1965. The crowning achievement of the Civil Rights Movement to that moment. Everyday people had put down their lives for it, and the main blow that we struck with the law was aimed at states and counties that had done their worst to keep black citizens from voting. Missis-sippi, for example, would ask black people coming to vote how many bubbles in a bar of soap, and they had to answer it before they could vote.

Congress passed the Voting Rights Act by an over-whelming margin, and it worked. Congress renewed it four times under Presidents Nixon, Ford, Reagan and the first George Bush. But forty-eight years later, after LBJ had signed it, the conservative majority on the court struck down key provisions of the act by a five to four vote.

I will never forget, because that was the case before the court that was the closest to my heart and experience. I will never forget the fiery dissent you wrote, describing discrimination against voters, "A vile infection," and denouncing and denouncing what you call the demolition of the Voting Rights Act.

You predicted, if you will remember, in that opinion that bad things would come from it, in the form of new and more sophisticated discrimination. And they have. This year stringent ID laws, new and more sophisticated purges of the voter rolls. The early closing of polls. Moving polls to out of the way places. Hard to reach. The majority's opinion in that case, Justice Ginsburg, has done enormous harm. Do you think the justices know this?

GINSBURG: Do I think they know it? Yes, but the majority placed the blame elsewhere. Perhaps we should explain the mechanism of the Voting Rights Act of 1965, states that had kept African Americans from the polls were put under a pre-clearance system. That meant if they wanted to make any change at all in their voting laws, they would have to have it pre-cleared by the civil rights division of the Department of Justice or a three judge district court in the District of Columbia. That meant that these repressive, restrictive laws never got passed, because the Department of Justice civil rights division would say, "No. We won't pre-clear this."

The majority's view was Voting Rights Act is 1965. We're now 2000-something. The formula is obsolete, because some of the places that discriminated in the past, some of the cities, some of the counties, are now up to snuff. So they shouldn't be under the system. "So Congress, redo the formula so that people subject to pre-clearance are the ones who deserve to be, who are still discriminating against African American voters."

Well, the stark reality, political reality, is a Congress that the Voting Rights Act had been recently renewed when the case came to the court. What member of Congress was going to stand up and say, "My district or my county or my city or my state is still discriminating, so keep us under the pre-clearance system." It wasn't going to happen. There wasn't going to be a new formula.

The act itself had a get out free mechanism. That is if you had a clean record for X number of years, you could bail out and you would no longer be subject to the pre-clearance system. So Congress saw the problem. It had provided the bail out, which I thought was the right way to do it. The political reality was Congress was not going to pass a new formula.

And I did say this is a law that really worked. That pre-clearance system worked. And it didn't come later. It came immediately. As soon as the heart of the Act was declared unconstitutional, you started to see these restrictive measures. The ones you mentioned. End the polling early in the day. Put them in far away places. Voter IDs.

MOYERS: You know, if I may, just hours after the court issued its judgment, Texas, the legislature of Texas, passed a severe

ID—well, the same day. Just hours after that. My friend Don Reeves called me and said, "Well, it's started." "What's started?" "The reversing." He would have said, "The arc is being pushed back the other direction." And you anticipated that. Was it some intuition you had?

GINSBURG: No. I think it was almost certain that that was going to happen. But the majority blamed Congress. Said, "This is legislation. The legislator should fix the statute so that it fits the contemporary scene, and not the scene in 1965." That was the court's view.

MOYERS: The case was decided when Obama was president, at a time when many Americans thought we were living in a post-racial America. We've been disabused of that notion in the past few years. And I want to ask you, do you think that if the opportunity came again, especially in the light of the bad fruit that this decision yielded, that the court might reconsider?

GINSBURG: Your crystal ball is as good as mine. I can only say I hope so. When I wrote that dissent, I was hoping that I could peel off one person from the majority. Didn't work out that—but every time I write a dissent hope springs eternal. And I'm thinking that I will—

MOYERS: Keep sounding the theme. Very quickly, what are the circumstances under which a court can reconsider? The court can reconsider a case?

GINSBURG: Well, this case will not be reconsidered, because the law is off the books now.

MOYERS: Right.

GINSBURG: It was declared unconstitutional, so it would be up to Congress, and I have no hope at all that the current Congress would redo the Voting Rights Act.

MOYERS: That makes two of us. It will not surprise you, of course, that the people here tonight are deeply engaged with religion in democracy. So I'd like to talk briefly about that. You have been a staunch defender of the separation of church and state. Why has that been so important to you?

GINSBURG: I think that religion is stronger when it's separate. When government isn't entangling itself with religion. I should say that the wall, to be frank, no longer exists. The current court has a different notion of what the religion clause, the establishment clause, free exercise clause what they mean.

And the notion is the state must be neutral among religions. So example, if there's a state support of Catholic parochial schools, there must be support for Jewish day schools as well. So the state can't pick and choose. They can have no preferred religion. But it's no longer the doctrine that the government must keep its hands off the church by not funding church-sponsored activities.

MOYERS: For a long time, the court recognized that the principle of religious freedom, liberty should be a shield to protect the exercise of religion, but it shouldn't be weaponized as a license to discriminate. So help us understand, those of us here tonight, the moral balancing act that the court engages in when reviewing a case where, say, your free exercise of religion collides with my free exercise of religion, because we believe differently or one of us may not believe at all. And I'm going to come to the—I'm not asking you to comment on any pending case, but we'll come to the Hobby Lobby decision in just a moment. What do you all consider as you try to balance these forces of church and state in your conferences?

GINSBURG: Well, one is a free exercise. The government should not interfere with someone's free exercise. And those cases are still I think solid. There was one case involving—I don't remember the name of the church, but they had animal sacrifice as their—

MOYERS: Yes.

GINSBURG: —ritual.

MOYERS: Kansas, I think.

GINSBURG: And the court allowed that free exercise. Now, you can go to extreme. There was a case when I was on the court of appeals. The church was called the Ethiopian Zion Coptic Church that had as its sacrament marijuana. But it was just not in church on a Sunday. It was all day, every day.

And so this church wanted to be licensed to import as much marijuana as it pleased so the members of its congregation could smoke marijuana all day, every day. I was surprised that that turned out to be a two to one decision. I wrote the decision saying no. But there was one of my colleagues who said, "If that's their belief, if that's their sacrament?"

MOYERS: You delivered another stinging dissent in the Hobby Lobby case. That's when the conservative majority owned the court by five to four. Decision ruled that because of their religious beliefs, the Christian owners of the company, Hobby Lobby, do not have to provide insurance coverage for birth control and contraception to their employees. And you call that decision a startling breath. Why that choice?

GINSBURG: Yes. The owner's free exercise right of their belief is something that I respect. But they had a workforce of people who were not of the same belief. And the federal law guaranteed to women insurance coverage had to cover contraceptives. And that the owners had a belief that contraception is sinful. They could have that belief, and as long as only co-religionists worked for them, it would be fine, because the women wouldn't ask for it.

But they were employing women who were of a different belief. Religious-based or not. And the owners are in business, in commerce. They have to abide by the rules that govern everybody, and should not be in a position of thrusting the way they believe on a workforce that doesn't share their beliefs. That was—

MOYERS: So you said, "The court I fear has walked into a minefield."

GINSBURG: Yes.

MOYERS: Explain that.

GINSBURG: Yes. Yes, it was understood that if you were engaged in a business selling to the public, you couldn't, for example, say, "I don't want to sell to Jews," or, "I don't want to sell to African Americans." You're in business. Your business has to be open to all people who want access to the facilities. That's very reasonable legislation to adopt. And that's the way it had been until—

MOYERS: Until—

GINSBURG: —Hobby Lobby, giving the owner the prerogative. Now, there were many, many cases along the way where there was a deeply held religious belief, but it couldn't be accommodated. Think of the Orthodox Jews who said, "We'd like to remain open on Sunday, because we must close on Saturday." That case came to the Warren court and they rejected the plea from the Orthodox Jews that they should be allowed to open on Sunday when all their competitors were closed.

MOYERS: Well, I grew up in this small town I was telling you about. Members of my church owned two drug stores with soda fountains in them. And both of them believed that segregation was ordained by the Bible, and that they didn't have to serve the black people of our town who came in. And that prevailed up until the '60s when we passed the Civil Rights Act of '65, which we talked about last week. So in effect—

GINSBURG: But I just, on that subject, would like to speak about a woman who came to be a role model for me, although we were both adults. In fact she was I think in one of the first groups of Episcopal ministers to be ordained. Her name was Pauli Murray.

MOYERS: Yes. Yes. That's right.

GINSBURG: And Pauli was attending Howard Law School in the middle '40s. All of the lunch pieces surrounding Howard University were white-only. Pauli in the '40s organized the Howard students to sit in at those lunch places, and all of the lunch places around Howard changed to admit the Howard students. That was Pauli in the '40s.

Before Howard, she was attending Hunter College here in the city, and she took one of her friends, a white woman, to go with her to visit her family in North Carolina. They crossed the Mason-Dixon line. Pauli is told to go to the back of the bus. She refuses and she's arrested in the '40s. Long before we heard of Rosa Parks. And she wrote an article that was a major influence on me and other women in the '70s. It was called "Jane Crow—"

MOYERS: Jane Crow?

GINSBURG: "—and the Law." Yeah. In which she spoke about all the barriers. The artificial barriers that stand in the way of women being able to achieve what their talent and hard work would allow them to achieve. She is finally—I think one of the residences at Yale, where she got her divinity degree, has been named—there was a name of a Southern slave owner on the building, and now it's named after Pauli Murray. And she was a woman way ahead of her time—

MOYERS: Way ahead of her time. So Michelle Alexander, if you're here, you have your next book. Jane Crow. Right?

GINSBURG: Jane Crow has been written by Rosalyn Rosenberg. It's been—

MOYERS: Yes.

GINSBURG: It's a biography of Pauli.

MOYERS: I love what you told Jeffrey Rosen, and Jeffrey Rosen was your collaborator in this new book, *Conversations with RBG*. Let's see. Love, law. Yeah, the two, liberty. Something else. But you said to him, quote—and this reminds me of that lean, muscular prose that you I think must have developed at Cornell.
  "Hobby Lobby was in business for profit. It employed hundreds of women who did not share those religious beliefs. So if you're going to employ people, a diverse workforce, you cannot force your belief on the peoples who work for you."
  "If that's a choice you want to make, if you want to be in business, then you have to play by the rules that all other businesses play by, and you can't disadvantage the people who work for you based on your belief, which they do not share." But we lost this round. You lost this round.

GINSBURG: Uh-huh.

MOYERS: And I was reminded that you had said elsewhere that the court has to be careful to see that Congress is not treading on our most fundamental human values. But I ask you who is going to see that the court does not tread on our fundamental values?

GINSBURG: The people who have controversies that will come before the court. The lawyers who will represent them. The commentators on the cases that the court will hear.

MOYERS: We the people?

GINSBURG: It has to start with we the people. There was a great jurist, although never on the Supreme Court. He's I think universally recognized as one of the great US jurists of all time, Learned Hand, who said, "If liberty is lost in the hearts of men and women, no court can restore it."

So almost every major change that we have seen has been the result of a groundswell of people saying, "What we have is not right. It needs to be changed." Think of how the gay rights movement changed when people came out of the closet and said, "This is who I am. I'm proud of it." The change was swift after that, but when people were hiding who they were—

MOYERS: Right.

GINSBURG: —nothing was happening.

MOYERS: I remember when the Civil Rights Movement, for which so many everyday people had died in the South and elsewhere, fortunately met with its deep thirst a political establishment in Washington, Congress and the White House, that held the hose that could satisfy that thrust.

That didn't happen with the gay rights movement until much later, but it finally happened. It was people who forced the change. Happened with the #MeToo movement. Started out there. It takes that combustion of ground moral power and political courage and wisdom, and the ability of the system, the courts and others, to move in sync, almost, to relieve longstanding—

GINSBURG: Well, I think the people start it. The court is a reactive institution, and it doesn't have a platform. Doesn't say, "This year we're gonna deal with this or that issue." It takes the complaints that are out there. So it has to start with the people, and if the people don't care, nothing is gonna happen.

MOYERS: I urge all of you to read a seminal article that the Justice wrote, which is in the book *In My Own Words?*

GINSBURG: *My Own.*

MOYERS: *My Own Words*. It's a wonderful collection, a different one from Rosen's book, but wonderful collection of her opinions and her articles and her speeches and her lectures. And in it you refer to the Supreme Court constitutional mistakes by which I assume you mean, for example, Dred Scott and *Plessy v. Ferguson*. It's clear from reading that, that many

of the constitutional issues the court has to decide entail argu-
able public policy choices. When the majority makes a choice
that you disagree with, do you consider yourself bound?

GINSBURG: It depends on the type of case. Most of the cases
we hear are not the heady constitutional variety but they're
interpretation of statutes. So let's say as a provision of the
internal revenue code, I think the taxpayer should have won,
but the court holds that the government wins.

That's eminently fixable by Congress. Congress knows
what the court held. It doesn't amend the law. So be it. In
that kind of case, I will say, "I was on the other side, but this
is how the court ruled. And it's up to Congress to change it, if
it wants to." I don't take the same view of key constitutional
questions, and I continue to disagree with the majority when
I think it has been egregiously wrong.

MOYERS: Is that why you sometimes read your dissents from
the bench instead of issuing them first in writing?

GINSBURG: Well, it's not instead of. It's in addition to.

MOYERS: In addition to.

GINSBURG: Usually. But when a case is decided the writer
of the majority opinion will read a summary of the opinion from the bench. And then we'll note, "Justice so and
so, joined by justices so and so dissent." That's it. One or
two times a year, sometimes four, sometimes none, when I
think the court not only got it wrong, but egregiously so, I

want to call attention to my dissent. So I will summarize it from the bench. I'm not going to re-bore someone by reading twenty pages, but within five minutes. So, for example, Shelby county was such a case. Hobby Lobby was another such a case. Lilly Led—

MOYERS: Lilly Ledbetter.

GINSBURG: Lilly Ledbetter.

MOYERS: Lilly Ledbetter. The case of Lilly Ledbetter is the one I would nominate for an Oscar for its drama.

GINSBURG: Yes.

MOYERS: Starring Ruth Bader Ginsburg.

GINSBURG: Sorry, Lilly.

MOYERS: It's classic—

GINSBURG: Lilly Ledbetter.

MOYERS: It's classic Ginsburg. A working woman named Letty—

GINSBURG: Lilly.

MOYERS: Lilly Ledbetter had sued Goodyear Tire and Rubber Company for back wages. When she discovered she had worked for years without being paid what men were paid for doing the same work. And if I'm correct, the court decided five to four that whatever the merit of the pay was concerned, she had waited too long to file her claim.

GINSBURG: Well, the law said you must complain of the discriminatory act within 180 days of its occurrence. And the court's view was, "Lilly, you're coming to us 12 years after you were engaged? You're way out of time." The dissent had a very simple notion. It's that the pay disparity was incorporated in every paycheck she received, so it's not that the discrimination happened and that it was over. It was continuing. And every time she received a paycheck, she had a renewed 180 days in which to sue.

That's what Congress adopted in the Lilly Ledbetter Fair Pay Act. The paycheck rule. If the employer has been discriminating and the discrimination is kept up, every time she gets a paycheck, the discrimination is renewed. But what I tried to get across in my dissent was Lilly was doing a job that up until then had been done predominantly by men.

She doesn't wanna be a troublemaker. She doesn't wanna rock the boat. The employer doesn't give out pay figures. But suppose somehow she had brought a suit early on. The defense almost certainly would have been—it has nothing to do with Lilly being a woman. She just doesn't do the job as well as the men, so we pay her less.

Now, advance a dozen or so years. They have been giving her good performance ratings all along. So now the defense that she doesn't do the job as well as the men, that's out, because she's been rated higher than the men. She has a winnable case. The court said she sued too late.

Well, it was a very short order that Congress, with large majorities, both Republican and Democrat, passed that measure. It was kind of a replay of what happened in the '70s when the court decided that discrimination on the basis of pregnancy is not discrimination on the basis of sex.

The reason the world is divided into non-pregnant people. That's most of us. Most men. Most women. All men. All men and most women. But then there's these people, these pregnant people, and there's no male counterpart. So whatever it is, it's not sex discrimination. So Congress in 1978 passed the Pregnancy Discrimination Act. The soul of simplicity. Discrimination on the basis of pregnancy is discrimination on the basis of sex.

Those decisions, Gilbert in the '70s, and Lilly Ledbetter's case many years later, it just caught the public attention and it said, "Where are they to say discrimination on the basis of pregnancy isn't discrimination?" And then the same thing in Lilly Ledbetter.

MOYERS: Well, the reason I mention the drama in Lilly is because you did forcefully read your dissent on the bench, and for some reason or the other, modern technology or wafting in the breeze, Barack Obama heard it.

GINSBURG: Well, but my tagline, the very last line in the dissent, was the ball is now in Congress's court to correct the error into which my colleagues have fallen.

MOYERS: Well, and the very first bill that Barack Obama signed when he arrived at the White House was the Lilly Ledbetter Pay—

GINSBURG: Fair Pay Act.

MOYERS: Fair Pay Act. And that's what I meant by the drama. It goes with the metaphor of the umbrella you used in the Shelby county case, which I know you must have written down when you were at Cornell and remembered it many years later. You remember it?

GINSBURG: Yes. It's—

MOYERS: Tell us.

GINSBURG: It says something to the effect of—

MOYERS: Throwing out—

GINSBURG: —saying

MOYERS: —pre-clearance. Throwing out—

GINSBURG: Yes, which has worked so well. It's, like, tossing away your umbrella in a rainstorm because you haven't been getting wet.

MOYERS: And someone wrote analyzing your experience at Cornell—wonderful essay by the way. I think it may have been Jeffrey Toobin. Our friend Jeffrey Toobin. Someone wrote that, "The image of using an umbrella in a rainstorm perfectly describes how the Voting Rights Act protected citizens in parts of the country where discrimination has prevented more than one minority group from voting. Easily visualized and easily remembered." I think the author of *Lolita* might well be applauding that line.

In your lecture on speaking in a judicial voice, and your good friend and mine and Judith's, Bill Josephson, who's sitting right there on the front row reminded me of this. You write about the importance of civility and respect among judges and justices. That that is, as you have said, one of the hallmarks of the court, collegiality.

But I'm wondering when your conservative colleagues rule in a way that diminishes the country as you see it, rules, say, that set women back or that leads to the suppression of votes, or to the execution of someone on death row, don't you feel some outrage? And do you ever express that outrage?

GINSBURG: Well, you've quoted from some of my dissenting opinions, but I'll use a phrase that my colleague, Nino Scalia used again and again, which is, "Get over it." And I can think—and the most vivid memory I have is of the *Bush v. Gore* case, where we divided sharply five to four.

But it was a marathon. We accepted the case on a Saturday. Briefs were filed on Sunday. Oral argument on Monday. Decision out Tuesday. So it was around the clock work for all of us. And the ones who were among the four, we were disappointed.

But we soon went into the January sitting and we had to

reason together. So we got over it. I sent my law clerks down to Justice Kennedy's chambers. He was on the other side. He wrote the principal opinion for Bush. And I wanted them to watch how the media was portraying this with Justice Kennedy's clerks. Justice Scalia called me about 9:00 that evening and said, "Ruth, what are you doing still at the court? You should go home and take a hot bath."

It is the most collegial place I've ever worked. And even though I can be disappointed, sorely disappointed in a colleague one day, I know we have to go on to some very important work the next day. So that we couldn't work as we do if we didn't maintain that collegiality.

MOYERS: But did he very get under your skin? Nino?

GINSBURG: Yeah.

MOYERS: I mean did you ever try to restrain some of his verbal—

GINSBURG: Yes.

MOYERS: —exercise—you did?

GINSBURG: And he helped me, because Justice Scalia was an expert grammarian. And every once in a while I'd make a grammatical error. He never embarrassed me by sending a note to the court saying, "Change this." He would either come to my chambers or call me on the phone.

I've many times said, "This is so strident. You'd be more

persuasive if you toned it down." And that was advice he never took. But to give you another example of collegiality. So one case where we divided sharply was the Virginia Military Institute case.

MOYERS: That's when you admitted women to what had been an all male—

GINSBURG: Right.

MOYERS: —academy in Virginia.

GINSBURG: So the court, there were only eight members participating, because Justice Thomas's son was attending VMI, so he was recused. Scalia ended up the lone dissenter. He came to my chambers and he threw down a sheaf of paper and said, "Ruth, I'm not yet ready to circulate this dissent to the full court. It still needs more polishing. But I want you to have it as early as I can give it to you so you'll have more time to answer it."

So I took his penultimate draft of his dissent on a plane with me and was going to a judicial conference. I read it and it ruined my weekend, but I was glad to have the extra time. And I'm also very pleased to say how wrong time has proved him to be. VMI has been a tremendous success story. The school has hardly gone to rack and ruin. It's gotten better in every way, and they're very proud of their women cadets.

MOYERS: I'm so impressed that you don't deal in abstractions, but you remember the people for whom those decisions

meant a different life or a different way of life. A different
chance in life. Whether it was Sally Reed. I believe she was
the first that was in the case—

GINSBURG: Oh, Sharron Frontiero Cohen. Who will be with
me in Omaha, Nebraska this summer. And it's a celebration
of the centennial of the Nineteenth Amendment. The amendment that gave women the right to vote. So Sharron, whose
case was the first one I actually argued in the court, will be
there. I've stayed in touch with her over the years.

MOYERS: Do you remember Wiesenfeld—

GINSBURG: Yes. In fact his son is coming to see me—

MOYERS: Wiesenfeld's son?

GINSBURG: Yeah. He spells it WEESEN-feld, but pro-
nounces it WISEN-feld. Why, I don't know. This is a man
whose wife died in childbirth, and he vowed that he would
work only part-time so that he could care personally for his
infant. There were Social Security benefits for the survivor
of a wage earner.

　　You could earn up to the earnings limit, put together
the Social Security and the part-time earnings, you could just
about make it to support yourself and the child. So Stephen
Wiesenfeld went to the Social Security office to claim what he
thought were child-in-care benefits. He was told, "We're very
sorry. These are mother's benefits, not father's."

So that was a case in which the court was unanimous in the judgment, but divided three ways on the reason. The majority said, "Obviously, the discrimination begins with the woman as wage earner. She pays the same Social Security taxes as the men. She doesn't get a discount on the taxes she owes, but her family doesn't get the same protection from the Social Security system."

Some, including my now-colleague John Paul Stevens, my recent colleague, said, "This is discrimination against the male as parent, because he doesn't have the opportunity to personally raise his child. He has to employ a substitute for himself so he can make the money needed to support the family."

And then there was one, and it was the first and the only time in the '70s where my later chief voted at least for the judgment that I was seeking, and that was then-Justice Rehnquist who said, "This is totally arbitrary from the point of view of the baby. Why should the baby have the opportunity to be cared for by a sole surviving parent only if the parent is female and not if that parent is male?"

MOYERS: Well, I'm going to get a sizzling dissent from this, I know, but I yielded some of our time to Serene and Judith. And I'm now only halfway through the interview, but I'm receiving a wrap notice over here from our director. I was going on to talk about the Nineteenth Amendment and where we are, and the fact that 100 years after women got the right to vote they still don't have equal political stature with men. Less than 25 percent of Congress is female.

GINSBURG: But then there were none when they—

MOYERS: Well, that's true. And I was gonna lay it out and— sexual harassment. Equal pay. All of that. But we don't have time. We'll come back to it. I was gonna talk about this re- markable issue of *Daedalus* journal, which is published by the American Academy of Arts and Sciences, updating us on where women are today. Really something I think you and everyone here will want to read.

I'm going to end with one question to which I ask you give me a brief answer, if you will. And it's because of who is here tonight. So many students who take very seriously their commitment to the moral imperative of faith that you do of the law. There's a saying that made the rounds in Washing- ton in the 1960s. "When injustice becomes law, resistance becomes duty."

And students from Union, faculty and staff as well, fre- quently take on injustice directly. They went to Ferguson. They went to Standing Rock. They've marched on the Capi- tol. They've sat down on the streets with Bill McKibbon and 350.org. What should citizens do, like these students have done, who see injustice being perpetrated?

GINSBURG: My faith is in today's young people. I've seen it in my granddaughter and the things that she is doing. In my former law clerks. One of my former law clerks is devoted to seeing to it that every child who turns 18 registers to vote. An organization that will take them to the polls.

My granddaughter is involved with the Purple Campaign, which is concerned with the sexual harassment in the workplace. I think there is a spirit among today's young people that wants to combat injustice. That's what I believe, and I would do everything I could to encourage that.

MOYERS: You've done your share. Justice Ginsburg, thank you very much.

RUTH BADER GINSBURG served on the Supreme Court of the United States as associate justice from 1993 until her death in 2020. Before that, she served on the US Court of Appeals for the District of Columbia Circuit from her appointment in 1980 by President Jimmy Carter until her appointment to the Supreme Court by President Bill Clinton. She graduated from Columbia Law School in 1959 in a tie for first in her class. She was on both the Columbia Law Review and the Harvard Law Review—the first woman to be on two major law reviews. She became a professor at Rutgers Law School in 1963 and she subsequently taught at Columbia Law School from 1972 to 1980. In 1972, she also co-founded the Women's Rights Project at the American Civil Liberties Union (ACLU). Through her work with the ACLU, she argued six gender discrimination cases before the Supreme Court between 1973 and 1976. She won five.

LESLEY OELSNER was a reporter and Washington correspondent for the *New York Times*, where she won a George Polk Award in 1972 for articles about court sentencing disparities. She covered legal affairs and the Supreme Court in Washington for the *Times* in the mid-1970s before serving as vice president and associate general counsel at Random House in Manhattan until September 2000.

CONNIE DOEBELE is a managing director for the Center for C-SPAN Scholarship and Engagement in the Brian Lamb School of Communication at Purdue University. She has more than twenty-five years of experience at C-SPAN, where she was involved in planning, implementing, and managing public affairs television programs as a senior executive producer.

MARVIN KALB is the Murrow professor emeritus at Harvard and hosts The Kalb Report at the National Press Club. He has been chief diplomatic correspondent for both CBS and NBC News, Moscow bureau chief, and anchor of NBC's "Meet the Press." Kalb went on to become founding director of Harvard University's Joan Shorenstein Center on the Press, Politics, and Public Policy.

NINA TOTENBERG is an American legal affairs correspondent for National Public Radio. Her reports air regularly on NPR's "All Things Considered," "Morning Edition," and "Weekend Edition."

JANE EISNER is writer-at-large at the *Forward*. For more than a decade, she was editor in chief of the *Forward*, the first woman to hold the position.

BILL MOYERS has been a broadcast journalist for more than four decades. He served as the ninth White House Press Secretary under the Johnson administration from 1965 to 1967. He was the publisher of *Newsday,* senior correspondent for CBS Reports, and later a senior news analyst for the CBS Evening News. He has also produced his own media programs: *NOW with Bill Moyers, Bill Moyers Journal,* and *Moyers & Company.*

THE LAST INTERVIEW SERIES

**KURT VONNEGUT:
THE LAST INTERVIEW**

$15.95 / $17.95 CAN

978-1-61219-090-7
ebook: 978-1-61219-091-4

**RAY BRADBURY:
THE LAST INTERVIEW**

$15.95 / $15.95 CAN

978-1-61219-421-9
ebook: 978-1-61219-422-6

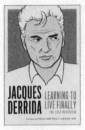

**JACQUES DERRIDA:
THE LAST INTERVIEW:
LEARNING TO LIVE
FINALLY**

$15.95 / $17.95 CAN

978-1-61219-094-5
ebook: 978-1-61219-032-7

**JAMES BALDWIN:
THE LAST INTERVIEW**

$15.95 / $15.95 CAN

978-1-61219-400-4
ebook: 978-1-61219-401-1

**ROBERTO BOLAÑO:
THE LAST INTERVIEW**

$15.95 / $17.95 CAN

978-1-61219-095-2
ebook: 978-1-61219-033-4

**GABRIEL GÁRCIA
MÁRQUEZ: THE LAST
INTERVIEW**

$15.95 / $15.95 CAN

978-1-61219-480-6
ebook: 978-1-61219-481-3

**JORGE LUIS BORGES:
THE LAST INTERVIEW**

$15.95 / $17.95 CAN

978-1-61219-204-8
ebook: 978-1-61219-205-5

**LOU REED:
THE LAST INTERVIEW**

$15.95 / $15.95 CAN

978-1-61219-478-3
ebook: 978-1-61219-479-0

**HANNAH ARENDT:
THE LAST INTERVIEW**

$15.95 / $15.95 CAN

978-1-61219-311-3
ebook: 978-1-61219-312-0

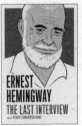

**ERNEST HEMINGWAY:
THE LAST INTERVIEW**

$15.95 / $20.95 CAN

978-1-61219-522-3
ebook: 978-1-61219-523-0

THE LAST INTERVIEW SERIES

PHILIP K. DICK:
THE LAST INTERVIEW

$15.95 / $20.95 CAN

978-1-61219-526-1
ebook: 978-1-61219-527-8

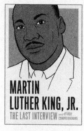

MARTIN LUTHER KING, JR.:
THE LAST INTERVIEW

$15.99 / $21.99 CAN

978-1-61219-616-9
ebook: 978-1-61219-617-6

NORA EPHRON:
THE LAST INTERVIEW

$15.95 / $20.95 CAN

978-1-61219-524-7
ebook: 978-1-61219-525-4

CHRISTOPHER HITCHENS:
THE LAST INTERVIEW

$15.99 / $20.99 CAN

978-1-61219-672-5
ebook: 978-1-61219-673-2

JANE JACOBS:
THE LAST INTERVIEW

$15.95 / $20.95 CAN

978-1-61219-534-6
ebook: 978-1-61219-535-3

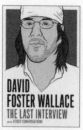

HUNTER S. THOMPSON:
THE LAST INTERVIEW

$15.99 / $20.99 CAN

978-1-61219-693-0
ebook: 978-1-61219-694-7

DAVID BOWIE:
THE LAST INTERVIEW

$16.99 / $22.99 CAN

978-1-61219-575-9
ebook: 978-1-61219-576-6

DAVID FOSTER WALLACE:
THE LAST INTERVIEW

$16.99 / 21.99 CAN

978-1-61219-741-8
ebook: 978-1-61219-742-5

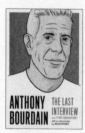

ANTHONY BOURDAIN:
THE LAST INTERVIEW

$16.99 / $22.99 CAN

978-1-61219-824-8
ebook: 978-1-61219-825-5

BILLIE HOLIDAY:
THE LAST INTERVIEW

$16.99 / 21.99 CAN

978-1-61219-741-8
ebook: 978-1-61219-742-5